Always remember where home is!
Love
Nancy Lou

BIRMINGHAM
THEN & NOW

BIRMINGHAM THEN & NOW

TODD KEITH

THUNDER BAY
P·R·E·S·S

San Diego, California

Thunder Bay Press
An imprint of the Advantage Publishers Group
10350 Barnes Canyon Road, San Diego, CA 92121
www.thunderbaybooks.com

Produced by Salamander Books,
an imprint of Anova Books Ltd.
10 Southcombe Street, London W14 0RA, UK

"Then and Now" is a registered trademark of Anova Books Ltd.

© 2008 Salamander Books

Library of Congress Cataloging-in-Publication Data

Keith, Todd, 1969-
  Birmingham then & now / Todd Keith.
    p. cm.
  Includes index.
  ISBN-13: 978-1-59223-949-8
  ISBN-10: 1-59223-949-8
  1. Birmingham (Ala.)--History--Pictorial works. 2. Birmingham (Ala.)--Pictorial works. 3. Birmingham
(Ala.)--Buildings, structures, etc.--Pictorial works. 4. Historic buildings--Alabama--Birmingham--Pictorial
works. I. Title. II. Title: Birmingham then and now.
  F334.B643K45 2009
  976.1'781--dc22
                          2008042431

1 2 3 4 5 13 12 11 10 09

Printed in China.

ACKNOWLEDGMENTS
Thanks to Jim Baggett, head of the Archives Department at Birmingham Public Library, as well as Don
Veasey and Yolanda Valtin for their patience and good humor when pestered with vague, arcane questions.
To Emily Kaple, whose diligent research assistance and meticulous approach to this project kept me on
track. To my underpaid live-in editor and wife, Julie. To Michael Calvert of Operation New Birmingham.
And to the Birmingham Historical Society for all their work. Finally, I'd like to acknowledge the
researchers, editors, and preservationists such as Marjorie L. White, Philip A. Morris, Carolyn Green
Satterfield, J. D. Weeks, James R. Bennett, and the many others whose diligent work documenting the
history of Birmingham and its people have made this project possible.

INTRODUCTION

Unlike cities that were founded based on their proximity to a port or important navigable river, Birmingham's beginnings lie squarely in the bedrock upon which it stands. Sitting at the southernmost end of the Appalachian Mountains, the city's topography is dominated by a valley and ridge formation running in a northwest-to-southwest direction. Beneath the hills lie two large coal reserves, the Warrior and Cahaba coalfields, named in 1848 by professor Michael Tuomey, the state's first geologist. Paired with a local abundance of iron ore and limestone, all the ingredients for making iron were at hand. Early observers remarked that the area was one of the few regions where corn and cotton grew over coal and iron. But cotton was never going to be the region's future.

Little more than a sparsely populated agricultural setting prior to the Civil War, the entire region of northern Alabama had a paltry seventeen forges, nine primitive furnaces, and one rolling mill producing iron. Yet the potential for manufacturing was clearly recognized, prompting the formation of the Elyton Land Company in Montgomery in 1870 by various capitalists and promoters of the region, who hoped to form a city in Jefferson County. Birmingham was incorporated in 1871. About a year later, Northern investors and local industrial interests, with the state's financial backing, finally completed the South and North Railroad in the area. After that, the railroads were Birmingham's rivers of commerce, and early business leaders like Henry DeBardeleben, James Sloss, and Charles Linn were its captains of industry.

Around this time, Elyton, or Ely's Town (located in Birmingham's West End today), had grown to approximately 1,000 residents. The lack of skilled labor, the nationwide financial panic of 1873, a shortage of capital, and a cholera epidemic in the new town slowed its initial growth, but Birmingham would quickly rebound to become an industrial powerhouse. By 1890 more than 20,000 people worked at the mines, furnaces, mills, and foundries dotting the county. By the end of the nineteenth century, Birmingham was the largest producer of iron in the world. The community had certainly earned its nickname of "the Magic City."

The tale has been told many times before, yet bears some repeating, if only because it is such a compelling one. Indeed, this magical tale of iron, steel, and industrial might became Birmingham's leitmotif for the first century of the city's existence. Famously, a sign on the old Chamber of Commerce building at the corner of First Avenue and Nineteenth Street downtown proclaimed, "Everything to Make Steel—Iron Ore, Coal and Limestone—Are All Within Gunshot of This Building."

And so it went with Birmingham's economy until after World War II, when the University of Alabama at Birmingham's medical school jump-started the region's health services and education industry that is today the state's single largest employer. Around the same time, Birmingham developed into the South's second-largest banking center, firmly anchoring the region's huge financial sector. And today, it is technology and the communications industry that are transforming the region yet again. Which brings us to the term "Birmingham."

Birmingham as an entity is problematic. When someone thinks "Birmingham," are they limiting themselves to the Birmingham municipal boundaries and the 230,000 people who live there? Communities such as Fairfield, Bessemer, Ensley, and Woodlawn were certainly part of what made the early city, while suburban "over the mountain" communities of the 1920s, such as Homewood and Mountain Brook, are the foundations of what now constitutes "Greater Birmingham," to use the phrase loosely. A thornier question is what to make of what is often called the Birmingham-Hoover Metropolitan Area, which, all told, encompasses two counties and has a population of over one million, roughly a quarter of the entire state's population.

For the purposes of this book—and despite of the massive recent growth of North Shelby County—I've focused on a more traditional and historic definition of Birmingham, perhaps stretching it a bit around the edges to include the early suburbs and communities. Yet, if 100 years from now another edition of this book is published, in all likelihood the rapid growth of Hoover and shrinking of Birmingham proper (in 1960 the city's population was 340,000) makes it possible that such a book might be called *Hoover-Birmingham Then and Now*.

Then again, recent trends could just as easily reverse the losses that the downtown endured in the past forty years. With new lofts, condos, and the refurbishment of dozens of previously vacant or underutilized buildings downtown, Birmingham's urban core is today more of a destination than at any time in the past thirty years. This coincides with the city's transformation from an industrial center to a more diversified economy. While high-profile businesses have left Birmingham for the suburbs—Trinity Medical Center, Red Diamond Coffee, and Southern Natural Gas Corporation come to mind as recent examples—at the same time, corporate entities such as Wachovia, Regions, Renasant Bank, Alagasco, Harbert Management Corporation, and others have specifically chosen downtown. Galleries, new hotels, upscale restaurants, and coffeehouses are opening their doors downtown rather than south of town. In one curious instance, the old Rialto Theatre was renovated and now operates a family business on the ground floor with a young family's residence above. This was nearly inconceivable even a decade ago.

One facet fueling this downtown energy and growth is the number of architectural treasures remaining. It is fairly surprising just how much of the architectural past still stands in Birmingham. Such a statement may come as a surprise to those familiar with Birmingham and the loss of such historic treasures as the Terminal Station, Tutwiler Hotel, and the old city hall. For anyone who doubts this, drive to Nashville or Atlanta, a metropolitan expanse with few traces of its past reflected among the high-rises and sprawl. Who would have guessed that the death throes of the steel industry and the deterioration of Birmingham's urban core in the 1960s and 1970s would leave behind such benefits?

Today, Birmingham is the most diversified city in the state, no longer relying primarily on the steel industry to generate jobs. From industries like banking and finance to publishing and health-related services and research, the city's landscape has changed and evolved dramatically. It is my hope that this book, which compares historic images of Birmingham with modern scenes, will further illuminate some of these exciting changes. For example, in the Birmingham of today, the number of people working in primary metals manufacturing constitute less than 1 percent of the workforce. Tell that to one of the thousands of hardworking miners or factory workers here 100 years ago, and they would look at you with a blank, uncomprehending expression. Yet, tell them that 50 percent of the cast-iron pipe produced in the United States is still made in the Magic City, and they would be suitably proud.

Looking east along a newly paved Bonita Drive in 1928, the striking new Spanish Colonial Revival–style homes being built are on display. For those in downtown Birmingham eager to live "over the mountain" in the newly developed suburbs, the young town of Hollywood was an obvious lure. Soon to be annexed into the greater town of Homewood in 1929, Hollywood featured lots that sold for $1,800 to $3,700. Completed homes on Bonita and nearby Poinciana Drive and La Prado Place typically went for $15,000 to $35,000. Well served by streetcars, much of the subdivision was developed by Clyde Nelson, whose curious slogan, "Out of the Smoke Zone, Into the Ozone," reveals just how unpleasant the steel-producing city's air quality could be at times. Architect George P. Turner designed many of the early houses in the then-fashionable style of Hollywood, California. The inset photo shows 207 (center) and 205 (far right) Bonita Drive.

Officially named the Hollywood Historic District and listed on the National Register of Historic Places in 2002, Hollywood continues to be a highly desired neighborhood because of its proximity to the city and the architectural style of its many Spanish and English Tudor-influenced homes. While a recent real estate boom meant that several houses on this street have been expanded, the original look and feel remains consistent with Clyde Nelson's original vision, largely because of the historic designation. Some of the wrought iron decorating the homes was purchased from New Orleans' French Quarter in the 1920s and dates back to Napoleonic France. A block to the west, the home of Hollywood's first and only mayor, Clarence Lloyd, still stands. The inset photo shows 205 Bonita Drive.

This photo, which was taken by Alvin Hudson around 1910, shows a collection of motorcycles assembled at the starting line of the Birmingham International Raceway on the grounds of the Alabama State Fairgrounds. The crowded stands can be seen at the left, as can the numerous spectators standing surrounding the track. The first Alabama State Fair was held in 1892 at this site near Five Points West, and the facility was later home to Kiddieland, an elaborate swimming pool facility, as well as a popular flea market. The statue of Vulcan can be seen faintly in the background—after the 1904 World's Fair, when no permanent site in Birmingham could be found for it, the fairgrounds became the statue's home. It resided there for almost three decades in ignominy: Vulcan's hammer wouldn't fit in his left hand because it was turned the wrong way, as was his right hand. Consequently, the god of fire held everything from a pickle sign to a Coca-Cola bottle.

Acquired by the City of Birmingham in 1947, the fairgrounds area and racetrack covers 117 acres. The State Fair Arena and Exposition building, built in 1980, holds 6,000 people and hosts sporting events, concerts, and conventions. However, around the turn of this century, the Alabama State Fair Authority went bankrupt due to a drop in attendance. In its newest incarnation—now called the Greater Alabama Fall Fair and Festival—a ten-day event at the fairgrounds again highlights agricultural and livestock accomplishments, arts, as well as commercial and industrial technology. After a long pedigree of stock car, motorcycle, and harness racing, in recent years the raceway has been home to high school football games and other events. The track and field has been condemned, and there are reportedly plans to dismantle the landmark.

Located just over Red Mountain, Homewood became one of the first streetcar suburbs of Birmingham when the Edgewood Electric Railway ran the first line from Five Points South in 1911. Looking south from Twenty-eighth Avenue South in 1930, one can see the Piggly Wiggly grocery store, still something of a Homewood landmark, albeit now located on Highway 31. A year earlier, Hollywood, Rosedale Park, Grove Park, and Edgewood merged to form the young city of Homewood, although the towns were considering joining the city of Birmingham instead. The inset photograph of Homewood Theatre was probably taken in 1928, the year that *While the City Sleeps*, the Lon Chaney feature, was released. The small sign above the door to the left of the theater marks the "colored entrance" to the balcony. Designed by Wilmot C. Douglas, the theater was located at 2834 Eighteenth Street South. It closed in the late 1950s.

Unlike many urban shopping districts in the Greater Birmingham area, Homewood's Eighteenth Street remains as vital today as it did during its inception. Until the early 2000s, the old site of Dunn's Pharmacy was still a drugstore. With 25,000 residents, Homewood has one of the highest population densities in Alabama, as well as a diverse racial makeup. Located one block east of Eighteenth Street, SoHo Square, a 265,000-square-foot development, features seventy-six condo units, a new city hall, retail shops, and underground parking. Completed in 2005, it is just one of several condo/loft projects reenergizing Homewood's central business district. After the old Homewood Theatre closed, the building held the Homewood Toy and Hobby Shop, a popular site for kids. Today, Homewood Cycle and Fitness, part of the Cahaba Cycles chain, occupies the building. The toy and hobby shop relocated next door.

Commissioned by the Commercial Club of Birmingham, the fifty-six-foot Vulcan statue was designed by Italian sculptor Giuseppe Moretti and is made of twenty-nine cast-iron components fashioned in 1903 by the Birmingham Steel and Iron Company. The head alone weighs 11,000 pounds. It won the grand prize at the 1904 Louisiana Purchase Exhibition in St. Louis. Vulcan is the largest cast-iron statue in the world. After a time at the Alabama State Fairgrounds, the god of fire and forge found a home atop Red Mountain (so named for the red iron ore used in the steel industry, seen exposed beneath the statue), thanks to a new park funded by the Works Progress Administration in 1936. With panoramic views of Birmingham, Vulcan Park has been an unofficial gathering place for visitors to Birmingham for decades. For more than fifty years, Vulcan held a green neon torch that was a familiar sight for commuters taking the Red Mountain Expressway: if there was a traffic fatality that day, the torch would be lit red. Vulcan was listed on the National Register of Historic Places in 1976.

After a massive $14 million renovation of the ten-acre urban green space from 1999 to 2004, the park reopened on Vulcan's 100th birthday, winning a National Preservation Honor Award from the National Trust for Historic Preservation. More than 100,000 visitors came to the park in its first year. A new Vulcan Center Museum tells the story of Birmingham's founding with displays and interactive exhibits interpreting the region's geology and suitability for iron production that was a key to Birmingham's early growth and development. A large ground map of the Birmingham region illustrates the location of iron ore, coal, and limestone that were vital for iron production. The site also hosts workshops, lectures, corporate and social events, as well as a popular summer outdoor music series called Vulcan AfterTunes. And of course, the old statue is once again the symbol of Birmingham.

In this 1929 view looking east into Mountain Brook Village, Mountain Brook Estates can be seen in the distance, as can a promotional sign showing a rendering of what the village will eventually resemble. Mountain Brook Estates, the crowning development of Robert Jemison Jr.'s Jemison and Company, was designed by Boston landscape architect Warren H. Manning to be the most exclusive subdivision in Birmingham—many of the lots were six times the size of the average city lot. Promotional materials for the Old English–style shopping center note the "superior types of business structures" planned, including parking spaces for automobiles as well as wide roads for safer travel during busy traffic. Mountain Brook was one of the first real-estate developments in the country to incorporate a shopping center. The development company built the first three buildings, but all subsequent structures had to earn the approval of Jemison and Company with regard to signage, awnings, and occupancy.

The Birmingham suburb of Mountain Brook, like the village shopping area of the same name, has continued to build on the fine pedigree that Jemison established. As befitting one of the country's most affluent communities, today Mountain Brook Village is replete with exclusive businesses such as Henry Maus Antiques, Barton Clay Jewelers, Susan G. Matthews, and other fine shops and galleries. Gilchrist Soda Shop occupies the building seen in the 1929 photo. The ubiquitous Starbucks—occupying the space behind where this photo was taken from Hollywood Boulevard—is the rare chain establishment. The area was originally called Watkin's Branch after landowner Daniel Watkins Jr. The name "Mountain Brook" was chosen by the developers in the 1920s. The chamber of commerce asserts that the first development in the United States to use the term "office park" was constructed here in 1952, continuing a tradition that Robert Jemison Jr. would be proud to claim. A strong sense of aesthetics, backed by building codes, has maintained the coherence of the village's original design.

Located on Shades Creek, the Old Mill was part of the larger Mountain Brook Estates plan that Robert Jemison Jr. developed on 400 wooded acres in Shades Valley starting in 1926. Built in the style of a nineteenth-century gristmill, the structure was conceived as a community clubhouse and a means to promote the new real-estate venture. In the language of a purple prose-laden advertising brochure, "Such is the setting, surpassed in natural charm by no other location in Birmingham, where Jemison and Company is fashioning today an exclusive estate section for country homes, where cultured persons can preserve those fine traditions of aristocratic country life which the Old South knew in antebellum days." The plan also called for a country club, golf course, riding academy, and miles of bridle trails. Designed by Birmingham landscape architect William H. Kessler, it was first operated as a tearoom by Frances Bomar until it closed during the Great Depression.

Located at 2780 Mountain Brook Parkway, the Old Mill became a private residence following the Depression and is today owned by the Henderson family. Not surprisingly, the Old Mill has been a popular subject for paintings and postcards since the 1930s. Enclosed in oak cladding and hand-split roof shakes, the interior contains a dramatic stone fireplace and pegged floors. In 2005 floods took out the pedestrian footbridge (not for the first time)

supported by stone piers, and the bridge was repaired using steel beams. The Jemison Park Nature Trail across the street is a popular gathering place for runners and walkers enjoying the woods and interpretative signs that illuminate area wildlife. A drawing of the Old Mill is depicted in the City of Mountain Brook's official seal.

This 1910 photo of the Robert Jemison Jr. house on Crescent Road in Mountain Terrace reveals perhaps the culmination of the Tudor-style residence. It includes an attic space that was used for dancing as well as a wine cellar. A signature feature of this forty-acre development—found just east of Lakeview Park along the north side of Red Mountain—was the gently curved roads and sidewalks that followed the contours of the land. Mountain Terrace was the first subdivision of this size to have paved streets and sidewalks, sewers, gaslights, and landscape plantings like crape myrtle, linden, and dogwood trees. Known as "Mr. Birmingham" because of his extensive involvement in the city's affairs, Jemison's business interests included real estate, insurance, and banking. Oscar W. Wells, a prominent local banker, purchased the house from Jemison in 1915 and lived there until his death in 1950.

Though the porch to the right has been closed in, the original awnings are gone, and the quaint wooden fence posts no longer stand adjacent to the sidewalk, the exterior of the house is largely the same today as it was almost a century ago. The semicircular driveway appears to have been expanded slightly, perhaps to better admit cars. After acquiring 300 additional acres next to and east of Mountain Terrace from the Avondale Land Company, Jemison sold the property to the Birmingham Realty Company, which then managed the exclusive properties. Now a part of Forest Park, the Mountain Terrace community remains one of the city's most desired addresses.

In 1921 Avondale Park was the scene of Birmingham's fiftieth anniversary celebrations where "The Pageant of Birmingham" was performed by a troupe of more than 100 singers and dancers—a sure sign of how intricately linked the park was with the young city. Taken around the time of the amphitheater's construction for the gala, this photo by O. V. Hunt shows a concert with those in attendance decked out in their best dress whites. Avondale Park was one of the city's premier recreation spots. The small collection of animals kept there in the early part of the century—including Miss Fancy, a former circus elephant—was the start of what would later become the Birmingham Zoo. The inset photo shows a Pizitz's department store Easter egg hunt held in the same spot in the 1940s, clearly an enormously popular activity.

Made of native sandstone, the small amphitheater at Avondale Park along the northern slope of Red Mountain has changed very little. The spring (once known as King's Spring) is still flowing, though it is no longer the water source for the surrounding homes. While perhaps not the urban destination it once was, Avondale Park and the amphitheater still host many sporting and cultural events such as Art in Avondale Park, an event geared toward inspiring children to discover their artistic talents through a variety of art lessons and activities. When Ruffner Mountain Park—one of the country's largest urban nature preserves—was dedicated in 1977, it eclipsed the forty-acre Avondale Park as the largest park in the city. In similar fashion, a recently proposed 1,108-acre Red Mountain Park on the east side of Birmingham may yet eclipse Ruffner Mountain Park in size.

Founded in 1898, the Country Club of Birmingham relocated to the Lakeview area, where it constructed a golf course that is the oldest in Alabama; it was later known as the Highland Park Club Golf and Country Club. The rustic Tudor-style clubhouse at Highland Avenue and Thirty-third Street was designed by architects John A. Miller and Hugh Martin and opened in 1904. It reportedly opened at six o'clock in the morning, closed at midnight seven days a week, and did not allow games to be played for money. This photograph from 1908 shows the front of the clubhouse and its well-manicured grounds. Located at the crest of the hill just below Red Mountain and what would become the exclusive Redmont Park community, the club enjoyed a wonderful view of the Lakeview neighborhood below.

In 1928 the club moved from their Highland location to what would become Mountain Brook when their growing membership necessitated a second eighteen-hole course. The property later passed into the hands of the City of Birmingham and was known as the Highland Park Club, and was the site of one of Bobby Jones's early victories at the age of fourteen. In 1955 the course was renamed for Birmingham native Charley Boswell, a seventeen-time National Blind Golf champion. Sadly, the old clubhouse and racquet club burned down in 1973, and was replaced with this decidedly modern architectural take. Today, it serves as the clubhouse for Highland Park tennis and golf, and also houses a tennis academy. In 1998 the Gold Course underwent a restoration.

A magnificent Gothic structure, the present Woodlawn High School was designed by architect Harry B. Wheelock and opened January 30, 1922—the previous high school was established six years earlier. A postcard from that time describes Birmingham's newest high school building as "Twenty-four instructors, 800 pupils. Cost of present unit and equipment $300,000." Sidney van Sheck and Richard Blauvelt Coe painted one of the largest Works Progress

Administration murals in the South around the auditorium's proscenium arch between 1934 and 1939. Woodlawn's legendary coach, John Blane, who spent fifty-three years at the school, cemented the school's sporting reputation early by leading the basketball team to state championships in 1927, 1937, 1943, and 1957, while the track team won championships in 1932, 1944, 1945, and 1946. Woodlawn also won three consecutive football titles from 1941 to 1943.

Today, Woodlawn is a magnet school that enrolls approximately 700 students. Notable alumni include Florida State University football coach Bobby Bowden, magician and children's show host "Cousin Cliff" Holman, author Paul Hemphill, and 2003 National Teacher of the Year Betsy Rogers. Like many historic communities in Birmingham, the loss of middle-class families and changing demographics dealt a heavy blow to urban schools and communities such as Woodlawn in the 1960s and 1970s. In the past decade, the structure's condition had deteriorated so badly that there was a talk of closing the school. The Montgomery architectural firm of Sherlock, Smith, and Adam was selected for the much-needed renovation, which was completed in 2007. Alumni of the school raised nearly $200,000 for the project.

Located at 5525 First Avenue North and Fifty-sixth Street, Woodlawn City Hall was built in 1909, approximately a year before this photograph was taken. In the picture, members of the Woodlawn Fire Department proudly pose on their new firefighting equipment behind the streetcar line. This city hall was the second built by the city; the first was completed in the mid-1890s when the population of the city reached 2,500. Incorporated in 1891, Woodlawn was named for Obadiah Wood, who settled in this section of Jones Valley in 1824 along the Georgia Road. In 1910 the Woodlawn community was annexed into Birmingham as part of the "Greater Birmingham" movement of the day that saw other communities such as Avondale, East Lake, West End, Ensley, and Wylam join Birmingham.

In the intervening decades, the old Woodlawn City Hall building has leased out its offices to a number of different businesses. While the elegant terra-cotta entry, the pair of Corinthian pilasters, and the full-gable pediment remain unchanged, the impressive octagonal cupola no longer sits atop the building. The building now houses the Eastside Funeral Home. Woodlawn had its share of tough times in the 1960s and 1970s, yet the strong sense of community for which the neighborhood was famous is still evident. Redevelopment efforts in

1985 intended to revitalize the community included tree planting, sidewalks, and street lighting. Today, Woodlawn is one of twenty-three Birmingham neighborhoods vested in the Community Participation Program, which seeks to facilitate local activism and involvement. Working with Region 2020 and the Community Foundation of Birmingham, Woodlawn is an important part of Birmingham's redevelopment plan, particularly the main residential area of Woodlawn along First Avenue North.

Long a Birmingham landmark, Quinlan Castle is a four-story apartment complex built in 1926 on Ninth Avenue South and Twenty-first Street South. Seen in this photo taken during construction, the building has a certain elegance that has intrigued passersby for generations. Designed by architect William C. Weston and built by H. P. Hanna, the building has a sandstone exterior and holds seventy-two small apartments. Arched windows, turrets at each corner, and battlements on the roofline add to the structure's character. It takes its name from Quinlan Avenue (the previous name of Ninth Avenue South), which was named after Bishop Quinlan of Mobile, who once owned the hilltop property.

A look at the present-day property quickly reveals a castle holding up poorly under siege. It is vacant, and its fate undecided. In 1940, however, Quinlan Castle went through a literal siege. Reputed to be the headquarters for Birmingham's Communist Party, it was raided by the police. Soon after, the much-maligned structure was renamed the Royal Arms Apartments. Added to the National Register of Historic Places in 1984, the building became property of the City of Birmingham in 1993. It is presently deteriorating, though the city has received a number of proposals for redevelopment. The city rejected a 1993 proposal by the neighboring Southern Research Institute to raze the building for a parking lot, and it appears that the historic shell at least will be saved regardless of what the future holds for the castle. It was added to the "Places in Peril" list of the Alabama Historical Commission in 1998.

So named for the streets joining here (Twentieth Street South, Magnolia Avenue South, and Eleventh Avenue South), which create five points, Five Points South has always been a hub of activity since the retail buildings' construction in the late 1920s. In this photo from that time, the Eleventh Avenue South block is seen finished in the popular Spanish style with its stuccoed facade and stone trim around arched doors. Topping off the lavish style is the red-glazed tile roof. The stores in the foreground included a post office, Peerless Laundry, and the Exchange Bank. Beginning in the spring of 1928 with capital of $35,000, the bank eventually moved to Tenth Avenue and Twentieth Street in 1947 and brought Birmingham its first drive-in teller window and bank parking lot. Exchange Bank became Exchange Security Bank in 1957, then finally Regions Bank.

Today, this section of Five Points remains as popular as when it was first developed. The private residence seen behind the laundry has long since vanished. That space is now an overflow parking lot for the many specialty shops, restaurants, and boutiques that populate the area. In the absence of the convenient streetcar line that once ran along Twentieth Street, the preference of the automobile over public transportation has had a great influence on downtown Birmingham. La Mesa Grill and Cantina now occupies the former laundry and bank space, while to the left, the popular Chez Fonfon is a casual, drop-in café that anchors Eleventh Avenue South along with Highland's Bar and Grill, its more famous neighbor.

By the early twentieth century, a busy electric streetcar line ran up and down Twentieth Street and through the circle at Five Points South, replacing the mule-drawn trolley. On December 2, 1903, the Five Points Methodist Episcopal Church, South (as it was then known) organized with a charter membership of 183 people, and within a year they purchased the site opposite the circle. The terra-cotta and brick Spanish Renaissance Revival–style sanctuary, seen here in the early 1930s, was completed in 1909. It was designed by Atlanta architect P. Thornton Marye, who also built the Birmingham Terminal Station as well as Atlanta's terminal and Fox Theatre. The bell tower at the left of the photo was not completed until 1921 due to insufficient funds. The Reverend Dr. Marvin Franklin was pastor at the time of this picture.

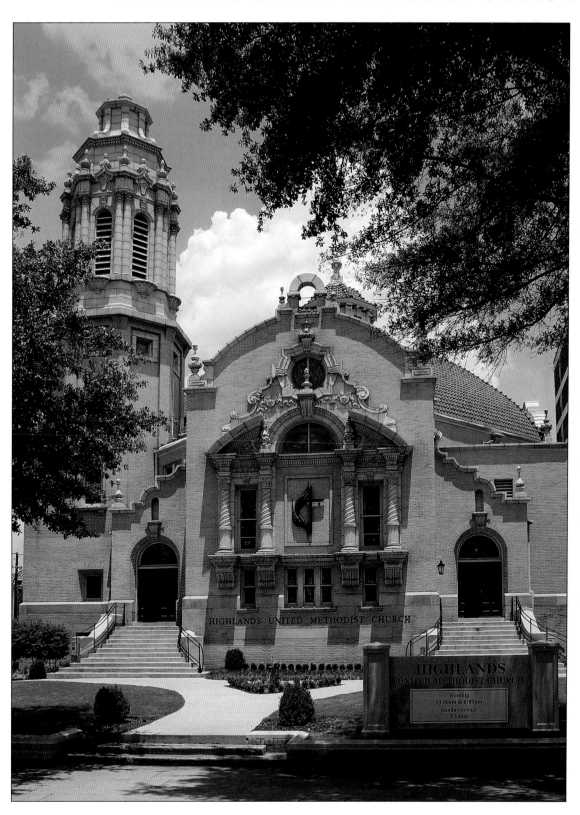

A Sunday school building was added to Highlands in 1924 in the Byzantine style. In the late 1940s, the sanctuary was turned around, making what was the back of the church the front. It was further remodeled, and the altar was moved into an addition to the sanctuary. Though the church witnessed the neighborhood's general decline in the 1970s—and the first decline in church attendance—Highlands remains involved in the community. The church actively supports such outreach programs as Habitat for Humanity, Community Garden, Urban Ministries in West End, and also operates a child-care center during the week. The McCoy Tower Bells, which are still run manually each Sunday before and after worship, were refurbished in 1995. The year 2003 marked Highlands' centennial, led by the Reverend Dr. Hughey Reynolds in the pulpit.

With its striking Venetian style and glazed polychrome terra-cotta, this retail block along Highland Avenue is an excellent example of the architectural look of many commercial buildings built in Birmingham during the late 1920s. The extensive details, reminiscent of the Florentine Building on Twenty-first Street at Second Avenue North, include the small corbeled arches and a false glazed-tile roof. The importance of the intersection can be seen in the streetcar lines, one running north on Twentieth Street to downtown or up the hill to the new suburbs of Homewood, and the other branching off to the left, heading toward Highland Avenue's residential areas. At the time of this photo, in the early 1930s, the Lyle Drug Company anchored the corner business block, along with a laundromat.

Like much of the Five Points neighborhood, this commercial block has seen its ups and downs. A sign touting Barber's Milk and Ice Cream accompanied by a clock later replaced the Buffalo Rock soda sign. The corner has housed a variety of businesses, including the Cadillac Café in the 1970s; a popular nightclub, Louis Louis, in the 1980s; and now the Bell Bottoms dance club. Over the years, as the area became more commercial, most of the large houses have been torn down to make way for offices or converted into apartments, and the streetcar lines are no longer present. Considering that Birmingham is the fiftieth-largest urbanized area in the United States yet ranks third in miles driven per person per day (34.8), there has recently been much discussion about re-creating the system of streetcars that worked so well for the city in the past.

Listed on the National Historic Register of Historic Places in 1986, the two-story neoclassical Bottega Favorita Building is found at 2240 Highland Avenue. Built in 1926 for the Gus Meyer Company as a department store, Miss Black Florists also shared space in the structure. At the time of this photo—not long after its construction—the Highlands neighborhood was still one of the city's prime residential areas. The building's designers, William Warren, Eugene Knight, and John Davis—three architects who left their mark on the city between the early 1900s to the 1950s—also drew the plans for the majestic Alabama Power Building. The Bottega Favorita Building has held many tenants over the years, including the Birmingham Area Boy Scouts, who used it for their headquarters.

In 1988 Birmingham restaurateur Frank Stitt opened the Bottega Restaurant in this historic building—a second addition to his family of restaurants in the area. A winner of the James Beard Award for "Best Chef of the Southeast," Stitt used this new culinary venture as a means to experiment with cuisines as diverse as Italian, North African, and Mediterranean. Two years later, he opened the Café at Bottega, patterned after Italian trattorias, on the right side of the building. In no time, the restaurants became a landmark, known for their flatbread pizzas, seafood, Parmesan soufflé, and their signature three-cheese macaroni and cheese. The outdoor patio is a bustling, popular destination for locals and visitors alike, and today the tiled roof, arched doors, and windows are as elegant as ever.

The Twenty-first Street viaduct seen in this photo (taken in 1919 during its construction) was the first major connection between downtown Birmingham and the Southside. It spans Morris Avenue, First Avenue South, and the railroad tracks, and is dedicated to the members of the 167th Infantry, Rainbow Division, who were killed in action in World War II. The regiment fought in battles such as Chateau Thierry, Sedan, Meuse-Argonne, and others—and was the only regiment to have two members be awarded the Medal of Honor during the war.

The Rainbow Division also participated in the capture of the first German prisoners taken by American soldiers during the war. In the foreground is the lumberyard of Chas T. Lehman's machinery shop, while downtown office buildings such as the white City Federal Building rise in the distance. On the viaduct itself, teams of horses can be seen putting the final touches on the new structure. It cost $160,000 to construct. The inset photo shows a view from the viaduct looking north in 1951.

While the surrounding skyline has risen since the viaduct's formal dedication on May 10, 1919, it is still immediately recognizable, anchored by the City Federal Building. In the distance behind it, Birmingham's banking nexus of Wachovia Bank, Regions Bank, and Compass Bank can be seen. Numerous warehouses with a view of the viaduct have been converted to lofts. Along an eight-block area of downtown along First Avenue South between Fourteenth and Eighteenth streets, the Railroad Park Foundation (formerly known as Friends of the Railroad District), began supervising the construction of the Railroad Park in 2007. A public/private collaboration, the park will include an amphitheater, a ten-acre open lawn, and an artificial lake, among other attributes. Future plans include developing the entire Railroad District that stretches from the former Alice Furnaces west of Interstate 65 to the Sloss Furnaces to the east and would include the area beneath the Rainbow Viaduct.

As Birmingham's first public school, Powell Elementary retains a special place for many longtime residents. It began as a simple two-story brick building with four classrooms in 1874, and was called the Free School, though students paid up to one dollar per year to attend, depending on their grade. Not long after Powell School opened, Birmingham's black community, led by Alfred Jackson, petitioned for a free black school, and the city complied, eventually establishing the Free Colored School. Named after Colonel James R. Powell (known as the "Duke of Birmingham"), Birmingham's first elected mayor, Powell School was rebuilt in 1888 on lots donated by Powell's Elyton Land Company. A cheerleader for the fledgling city and owner of much of the farmland that would eventually become Birmingham, Powell's vision for "our magic little industrial city" was transformative. This photo is from the early twentieth century.

Made of red brick, the three-story Victorian Gothic–style school enjoys high ceilings, thick walls, and the only fireplace still located in a Birmingham school. Still proudly persevering (minus the original tower) at its location at Sixth Avenue North and Twenty-fourth Street, in the 1940s a portion of a bond issue was used to add a lunchroom and additional classroom space to Powell Elementary. Additional modernizations brought the aging school up to current standards, but by the 1960s, there were discussions about tearing the building down. Preservationists won the argument. Listed on the National Register of Historic Places, Powell is the oldest school building in Birmingham. In 2002 Powell closed its doors as a school. Currently, the school district is considering selling the property. Proposals have been put forward for using the school as an archive or museum, but nothing has been determined for certain.

In 1872 the courthouse in Elyton burned, and at about the same time the nascent town of Birmingham took the county seat away from Elyton and constructed the Jefferson County Courthouse on the corner of Third Avenue and Twenty-first Street North. The photo above was taken shortly after its completion. The Italianate-style building was designed by architect W. K. Ball, and cost $30,500. After that structure was condemned and torn down in 1887, a new courthouse was completed on the same site in 1889. The elaborate and attractive three-story structure seen in the main photo had an imposing clock tower that stood 180 feet tall—a convenient lookout point for the fires that were always a threat. The four-story Romanesque brick building cost $300,000 to construct. A separate Bessemer Division of the circuit court was established in 1915 to handle cases from the western portion of the county. The twin spires of St. Paul's Cathedral can be seen far right.

The old courthouse served until 1931, shortly after the new and current Jefferson County Courthouse in the Linn Park municipal complex was completed. The building was razed and for decades served as a parking lot for the YMCA. Presently, the Concord Center office building occupies the spot. Completed in 2002, the eleven-story structure towers over Birmingham much the same way the old courthouse's clock tower did from the same spot. The building cost $25 million and holds 150,000 square feet. At the time of its announcement, it was the first multitenant office building built downtown in more than a decade. Williams-Blackstock Architects handled the design work while Bill Harbert Construction was the project's general contractor. In 2008 the Harbert Management Corporation relocated its 120-employee headquarters to the building.

Informally known as St. Paul's Cathedral, the church is located at 2120 Third Avenue North, just down the street from the site of Jefferson County's first two courthouses, now the site of the Concord Center. The first modest wood-frame church—thirty feet by sixty feet—stood adjacent to the present one and was built in 1872. It was Jefferson County's first Catholic church and occupied a lot donated by the Elyton Land Company. The imposing structure seen in this 1910 photo was constructed under the auspices of Reverend Patrick O'Reilly, the church's second pastor, and was dedicated on November 30, 1893, after more than three years of construction at a cost of $90,000. Gothic in style, the cathedral's pressed red bricks hold elaborate stained-glass windows. Its towering twin spires stand 183 feet above the ground—significantly, just a few feet taller than the nearby courthouse's bell tower. One cannot help but imagine that this gentle reminder to the cathedral's secular neighbor was not incidental.

In the 1920s, an anti-Catholic atmosphere in Birmingham was intensified by a politically active Ku Klux Klan. This culminated on the steps of the cathedral in 1921 when its pastor, Father James E. Coyle, was shot and killed by a Methodist preacher after his daughter became a Catholic and married a Catholic of Puerto Rican ancestry. Air-conditioning was added during extensive renovations in 1955. In 1972 some structural repairs were necessary, and the cathedral sanctuary was remodeled in accordance with the Second Vatican Council. Other remodeling was completed a few decades later to prepare for its centennial. Built in basilica form, ten granite columns support the arches and vaults, and its exterior measures 140 feet long by 96 feet wide. As befitting its urban presence, the cathedral supports a shelter for homeless people as well as a ministry for expectant women and young mothers.

First designated as "Park" on the original 1873 survey of the City of Birmingham, the park became Central Park to go with the other two parks, East (now Marconi) and West (now Kelly Ingram) parks. As part of an orchestrated campaign to relocate the state capital to this location from Montgomery, it was dubbed Capitol Park in the 1880s. Deeded to the city by the Elyton Land Company in 1883 on the condition that money be spent to improve it, by the last part of the century, elegant Victorian homes—some of the city's finest— surrounded the public space and a railroad line ran adjacent to the park. In this photo, taken during its Capitol Park era, one can see a host of newly planted trees and landscaping, the Confederate memorial in the foreground, and a statue of Dr. W. E. B. Davis visible at right. In 1918 it was renamed Woodrow Wilson Park, most likely because of a surge of patriotism following World War I.

After nearly a year of construction, the newly renovated and rechristened Linn Park opened in October 1988, paying tribute to Charles Linn, a Swedish sea captain and one of Birmingham's first industrialists. The $2.6 million venture introduced a central fountain and plaza with intricate brick and granite pavers. Designed by Nimrod Long and Associates, the transformation made the space a true urban refuge. Mature shade trees harbor workers on lunch breaks and provide an ideal site for events while also offering a natural escape for downtown residents. The site for City Stages, Operation New Birmingham's Magic City Art Connection, the Mercedes Marathon, and other events, Linn Park has become both a place of great symbolic and practical importance to the city. Today, two statues commemorating Birmingham's contributions to World War I flank the Confederate Monument. The Davis statue was relocated to the University of Alabama at Birmingham Medical Center in 1957.

In this charming photo taken in the early 1920s, a well-choreographed line of pickups is parked on the south side of what was then known as Woodrow Wilson Park. Arranged on Seventh Avenue North, each holds a pair of new Maytag washing machines, possibly new electric models. Maytag notices have been painted on the automobiles' side doors advertising for the House-Hold Appliance Company, which took the picture. At the left of the picture, some early Victorian residences can still be seen along Twentieth Street, though by this time the area was giving way to commercial structures at the expense of many beautiful homes. Two blocks down the street, the Molton Hotel was constructed in 1913 on land given to Mrs. Molton by her father, Charles Linn, whose name would later adorn the park.

Warren H. Manning, a renowned landscape architect from Boston, created a master plan for the city in 1919 that called for the park to be surrounded by public buildings in the Beaux Arts style. A 450-foot memorial to American war veterans was to be set at Twentieth Street, where this photograph was taken. While that grand scheme failed to come to fruition, when the Birmingham Park and Recreation Board hired the Olmsted brothers in 1923, the idea of the park's central importance to the city was firmly established. The Olmsted brothers devised a city master plan and designed several city parks. Twentieth Street would also be transformed into modern Birmingham's nexus of banking, with the Wachovia (formerly SouthTrust Bank), Regions (formerly AmSouth Bank), and Compass Bank towers seen in this view.

Birmingham's earliest church was a simple frame building with a Gothic roof built on the corner of Sixth Avenue North and Twentieth Street in 1873. It sat 200 people and faced Sixth Avenue behind where the current church stands. The choice site cost the new congregation five dollars. As the city grew, despite economic turmoil and a devastating cholera epidemic, so did the congregation—and in 1893, after six years of stop-and-start work on the new church, this wonderful structure of gray sandstone with its Romanesque columns and Gothic arches was finally completed. Architect Charles Wheelock, an early church member, oversaw the design. Known for its courtyard garden, other cathedral features of note are the oak-paneled doors, Grieb organ, and the crenellated buttressed bell tower. Taken in 1910, the photo shows some early residences that still remained in the area.

Known locally as "the Advent," the church's sermons and class audio are available by podcast or as online downloads, a sure sign of modern times. The church also runs the highly regarded Advent Episcopal School for kindergarten through eighth grade, and sponsors more than two dozen local outreach programs. The 3,800-member congregation is one of the largest Episcopal parishes in country, and serves as the cathedral for the Episcopal Diocese of Alabama. On the National Register of Historic Places, the church has been called "the Cradle of Bishops" because four previous rectors have become bishops. An extensive project to preserve and protect the church's sandstone exterior was completed in 2005, and today the church looks as resplendent as ever.

Built in 1914, the magnificent Tutwiler Hotel was the grand dame of Birmingham hotels for most of its sixty years. It was built by Robert Jemison to convince the American Iron and Steel Institute to hold its annual convention in Birmingham. Major Edward M. Tutwiler, owner of Tutwiler Coal, Coke and Iron Company, provided the financing and thus, the name. Its large and elegant lobby included a mezzanine balcony meant to impress guests with the size and scale of the hotel. It held 343 rooms, and the grand ballroom itself could host parties or meetings of 1,200 people. Nightly rates started at $1.50 for a single room without a bath. During Birmingham's annual Veterans Day Parade, the oldest such celebration in the country, the hotel constructed a popular reviewing stand so guests could observe the festivities. This photo from the 1920s reveals just how glorious the old hotel was. In the distance at left is the thirteen-story, 225-room Redmont Hotel, which was completed in 1925, and claimed to be the first hotel in the city with a "private bath in every room."

Between the 1930s and 1960s, the hotel would host conventions, wedding parties, and countless celebrations as well as notables such as Charles Lindbergh, actress Tallulah Bankhead, and President Warren G. Harding. Along with the Morris Hotel, the Terminal Station, and the Temple Theatre, the loss of the Tutwiler Hotel looms large among preservationists. In many ways, the Tutwiler helped establish Twentieth Street as Birmingham's main corridor, yet by the late 1950s, some of the hotel's grand sheen was fading. In the next few decades, ownership of the Tutwiler changed hands until the Great Southern Investment Corporation purchased the hotel. Yet in 1972, the Tutwiler closed its doors for good. It was imploded two years later to make way for the headquarters of First Alabama Bank, which today is known as Regions Bank. In 2007 Regions Bank announced that the seventeen-floor building would be redeveloped into a 255-room Marriott Renaissance hotel, a somewhat ironic turn of events. In the background, the Redmont Hotel remains the only hotel in this area still operating from the early part of the twentieth century.

This parade down Twentieth Street on May 10, 1919, welcomes home the famous infantry division of the Alabama National Guard known as the Rainbow Division. A World War II veteran, Raymond Weeks of Birmingham, is credited with having organized the first celebration using the term "Veterans Day." This celebration had its roots in an observance known as Armistice Day, which recognized the symbolic ending of World War I. The day was established in 1926 to pay respect to all the people across the world who had lost their lives fighting in the war. The fighting ceased at 11:00 a.m. on November 11, 1918—the eleventh hour of the eleventh day of the eleventh month. Weeks wanted to honor the people who served during World War II, so he organized the first Veterans Parade in Birmingham, which led to the passage of a congressional bill in 1954 renaming November 11 as Veterans Day in honor of all who served in the American armed forces.

Today, the traditions of the National Veterans Day Parade are still strong in Birmingham. The parade typically centers on a 1.5-mile route that includes Twentieth Street North and surrounding blocks, and features veteran organizations, Boy Scouts, Girl Scouts, military units, and various marching bands and school groups. Twentieth Street North is also known as Birmingham Green, a refurbishment of a seven-block area completed in the early 1970s to enhance the street with raised flower beds, tree plantings, and wide sidewalks, as seen in this photograph. Led by landscape architect Michael Kirk, it was one of the first such civic projects. The project cost $5 million, an amount paid for by local businesses as well as local and federal governments. Interestingly, MedTown Pharmacy currently occupies the corner of Twentieth Street and Third Avenue North, where there was also a drug store in 1918.

Chief among the more racy bits of Birmingham history is the story of Louise Wooster, better known as Lou, Birmingham's most successful and well-known madam. She gained fame for remaining in the city during the 1873 cholera epidemic and nursing many of the sick. In 1881 she purchased the two-story building at 1914 Fourth Avenue North that, in this circa-1912 photo, houses the Alabama Barber College. She later bought the building to the right (the Alabama Supply Company) to operate as her brothel and used the other building as her residence. Remarkably, the location placed her just across the street from Birmingham's city hall, a deliberate choice on the savvy Wooster's part. An able manager and successful businesswoman, Wooster prospered in this location, where she was able to count on local authorities for their tacit protection—she was brought into court only once.

After her retirement in 1901, Wooster kept these two buildings and rented them out to various businesses such as a laundry, jeweler, grocer, and liquor distributor. In 1911 she published *The Autobiography of a Magdalen*, a life story told as a cautionary tale, recently reprinted with an introduction by James L. Baggett as *A Woman of the Town*. Both of the buildings Wooster owned on Fourth Avenue were eventually torn down and replaced with a parking lot.

Today, one of the few visible signs of her existence comes in the form of one of the earliest downtown loft renovations, named Wooster Lofts in her honor. To the left of the parking lot is 1914 Fourth Avenue and to the right is the Clark Building at 1908 Fourth Avenue, formerly the Smith and Hardwick Bookstore. Both buildings are now the offices of the law firm of Lightfoot, Franklin and White.

Designed by architect Arthur G. Larson of Chicago, the elaborate and impressive Alabama Theatre opened on Christmas Day in 1927. Built by Paramount Studios to feature Paramount films, the 2,500-seat theater was known as "the Showplace of the South." Materials for its construction included French, Belgian, and Italian marble as well as terra-cotta from New York and granite from Minnesota. The facade was done in the Spanish Revival style with tall columns framing the three-story windows that preside over the entrance. Just across the street, on the corner of Eighteenth Street and Third Avenue North, stands the Lyric Theatre, built in 1914 as a vaudeville venue. It attracted performers such as Jack Benny, Will Rogers, Buster Keaton, Mae West, and other such luminaries. After the Great Depression, it reopened as a movie house, a role it still played in this 1948 photograph of the theater district.

In 1987 the owners of the Alabama Theatre declared bankruptcy and Birmingham Landmarks, Inc., a nonprofit corporation headed by Cecil Whitmire, purchased and oversaw fund-raising and a major restoration of the movie palace in 1998—all of the gold leaf paint was either cleaned or replaced, returning the showplace to its former grandeur. Now called the Alabama Theatre for the Performing Arts, it hosts live concerts, classic films, and musicals. Birmingham Landmarks

has also purchased the Lyric with plans to restore the historic five-story, 35,000-square-foot building as a performing-arts venue. It will be a welcome return to better days after several decades of neglect. Before closing in the early 1990s, the Lyric's last incarnation was as the less-than-respectable Foxy Adult Cinema.

Located at the corner of Third Avenue North and Nineteenth Street, the modernist S. H. Kress and Company Building was built in 1937, the year this photograph was taken. It appears that the first floor has been completed but the upper floors are still under construction. Pictures from later years show the large capital letters KRESS affixed to the marquee on the upper floors. It was known as a five-and-dime store and was a familiar sight in most cities across the country. The fine architecture of the various stores set them apart from most of their competitors. The original Kress store was on Second Avenue between Nineteenth and Twentieth streets and advertised its wares with a sign that read "5-10-25 Cent Store."

In 1978 the Kress department store closed. Known today as the Kress Building, the structure is listed on the National Register of Historic Places. After changing hands several times, the five-story, 75,000-square-foot building was purchased by the law firm Wiggins, Childs, Quinn and Pantazis, LLC, and renovated into new offices. Architects at Cohen and Company, Inc., designed the renovation. Work began in 2004 and the $7 million rehabilitation finished that same year. Great care was taken to maintain both the exterior and interior qualities, such as the pink marble staircase. The brass KRESS sign on the walls and roofline have also been preserved. With its white terra-cotta tiles restored to their original shine, it is easy to see why the building has been called the finest example of modern architecture in downtown Birmingham. The Watts Building can be seen in the background to the right.

Located on the corner of Second Avenue and Eighteenth Street, the Krystal Diner occupied the ground floor of this three-story parking deck downtown. Located around the corner from the theater district, patrons of the Lyric or Alabama theaters would enjoy items such as hamburgers and tenderized ham sandwiches for twenty-five cents, french-fried potatoes for fifteen cents, or homemade chili with beans for twenty cents. Right next door, the Dixie Cream Donut Shop made its hot, fresh treats another temptation for moviegoers. Perhaps less than appetizing is the Rideout's mortuary billboard prominently displayed just above the diner entrance. At the top of this photograph from the early 1950s, the Loveman's department store sign can be seen on what appears to be a water tower on the roof. Previously, Birmingham's first post office and customhouse, built in 1891, sat on this corner (inset).

Sadly, the Krystal Diner is a relic of the past, just as the old post office and customhouse were before it. However, repeating a theme in Birmingham and elsewhere, old historic structures came down in the postwar years, making way for parking lots, which were deemed more valuable than buildings as the automobile became the primary means of transportation. The post office was torn down in the 1920s for a dry-goods retail store that, because of the Depression's intervention, was never built. The site remained an empty lot until the parking deck was built. The towering parking deck presently at this location serves the adjacent McWane Science Center, Science Museum, Aquarium, and IMAX Dome, as well as special theatrical and musical events at the Alabama Theatre, which is located to the left of the deck. With its unusual tightly curving central ramp that ferries cars to their respective floors, the parking deck is something of a signature experience for kids of all ages.

This photograph looks down Seventeenth Street North from Fifth Avenue. It was taken on May 3, 1963, as Birmingham police and fire officers set up a cordon to block protesters coming up the street from the nearby Sixteenth Street Baptist Church. That same week, the infamous fire hoses and police dogs were turned on protest marchers in the adjacent Kelly Ingram Park. Arguably one of the more significant dates in modern Birmingham history occurred a couple of weeks earlier on April 16, 1963. On that day, while incarcerated, Martin Luther King Jr. wrote his "Letter from Birmingham Jail," an eloquent rejoinder to eight white clergymen in Alabama who urged him to call off the nonviolent protests against segregation in the city. King's reply to their insistence that he wait and fight the battle in the courts rather than on the streets brought about his famous response that civil disobedience is justified when confronted with unfair laws, and that, in fact, "one has a moral responsibility to disobey unjust laws."

Looking at the streetscape today, there are few physical signs of the turmoil and chaos of 1963. Yet those protests led directly to the passage of the Civil Rights Act of 1964 and other civil rights laws. Local merchants removed their "whites only" signs from their windows, lunch counters were desegregated, and the city's Jim Crow laws were soon repealed. Eventually, schools, libraries, and public buildings were desegregated. This area is now part of Birmingham's Civil Rights District. The Carver Theatre, now known as the Carver

Performing Arts Center, still stands in the distance along Fourth Avenue. After some hard times, it was remodeled in 1990 and today it no longer caters only to African Americans, serving as an important repository of Birmingham history and culture. It is also home to the Alabama Jazz Hall of Fame. To the right, Kelly Ingram Park (formerly West Park) occupies a full block, across from which lies the Birmingham Civil Rights Institute.

Founded in 1873 as the First Colored Baptist Church of Birmingham, this was the first black church to organize in the new city. It became Sixteenth Street Baptist Church after moving to this location in 1884. A previous building stood here but was condemned by the city, and the present building was constructed in 1911. Designed by African American architect Wallace Rayfield and built by local contractor T. C. Windham, the Romanesque and Byzantine-influenced design cost $26,000 to construct. As one of the primary churches for the black community, Sixteenth Street Baptist Church has played a pivotal role in Birmingham's history, not solely because of its prominence in the civil rights movement of the 1950s and 1960s. This photo was taken in the 1930s from across the street at Kelly Ingram Park.

Now listed by the National Park Service as a historical place of the civil rights movement, the church was a headquarters for meetings and rallies during that time. For many people, Sixteenth Street Baptist Church is forever linked with the morning of Sunday, September 15, 1963, when members of the Ku Klux Klan set off multiple sticks of dynamite in the church basement, killing four young girls and injuring many others. Remarkably, it wasn't until

2002 that the last living man responsible for the bombing was finally convicted of the crime. Today, the church is part of a larger civil rights district that includes Kelly Ingram Park and the Birmingham Civil Rights Institute, founded in 1992. Sixteenth Street Baptist Church is listed as a National Historic Landmark.

In this photo taken on May 16, 1963, Martin Luther King Jr. and a group of supporters in the civil rights struggle had just posted his appeal bond on a contempt citation in the Jefferson County Courthouse. Only three days earlier, President John F. Kennedy dispatched 3,000 federal troops to the city to quell riots, a move predictably protested by Alabama governor George Wallace, who announced his plans to sue the United States government over the use of troops. The eyes of the country, as well as the world, were fixed squarely on the demonstrations, protests, and police brutality occurring in the city. The nine-story modernist granite and limestone courthouse was built between 1929 and 1932, and was designed by the Chicago firm of Holabird and Root. It has wonderful panels over the entrance that reflect the state's early history, including Native American, French, Spanish, English, and Confederate, as well as more localized images of smokestacks and blast furnaces that presented a portrait of the city during the courthouse's construction.

A curious marker contrasting a romanticized Old South and an industrialized New South can be seen in the dramatic murals of John Norton in the courthouse lobby. Appropriately enough, an inscription in the limestone on the opposite side of the courthouse quotes Thomas Jefferson: "Equal and exact justice to all men of whatever state or persuasion." It took some time after the protests led by Martin Luther King Jr. and local leaders such as Reverend Fred Shuttlesworth to achieve this goal. Since that time, Woodrow

Wilson Park, the green space at the heart of the city's civic center, was renovated, renamed Linn Park, and reopened in 1988 after a $2.6 million project that, among other things, added a grand central fountain that had long been planned. The central plaza was formalized with patterned pavings of brick, granite seat walls and steps, along with an entertainment pavilion and other features.

This view of Fourth Avenue North in the early 1930s shows the black business district in its heyday. Looking west across Eighteenth Street North, an assortment of businesses such as the Brock Drug Company, Champion Theatre, Bob's Savoy, New Home Hotel, and others can be seen. By the 1910s, Fourth Avenue had become the commercial and social center for black citizens as the dictates of repressive Jim Crow laws enforced racial separation. Before this time, a black business district did not exist. Along the same street stand the Famous Theater and other landmarks like the towering Masonic Temple seen in the distance at right. The temple was not only the business and cultural life of the avenue, it also hosted social and athletic events, as well as big bands in its dance hall, including Duke Ellington, Jimmy Dorsey, and Count Basie.

On May 26, 1956, the padlocking of the National Association for the Advancement of Colored People offices in the Masonic Temple was a major contributor to the start of the civil rights movement in Birmingham. While hotels, barbershops, banks, theaters, and funeral homes thrived here until desegregation in the 1960s, the ensuing decades saw a period of decline for much of Fourth Avenue as racial zoning laws were discarded. By the 1990s, though, black businesses in the area began a small renaissance. Today, Urban Impact and the Alabama Jazz Hall of Fame produce an annual Taste of Fourth Avenue Jazz Festival at the historic Carver Theater, which was not built at the time of the 1930s photograph. On the corner at the left stands the Eddie Kendricks Memorial where the Brock Drugs Building used to be next to the Famous Theater. Across the street, the strip of businesses that include the New Home Hotel is now a small park with historical markers offering information about the district.

This lovely photo from around 1930 shows the Bradford Funeral Home on Seventh Avenue North. Ersie Bradford ran her business in several locations from 1908 until 1941. In 1936 Bradford reportedly became the first African American to serve on a Jefferson County jury. The house was constructed in 1910 and stands in clear contrast to the more simple structure at left. With its Romanesque stone arch, Queen Anne–style gable, and the classical columns, the house exhibits an unusual collection of influences.

While this stretch of Seventh Avenue has seen better days, recent developments in the Civil Rights District behind it have certainly improved the neighborhood. The Sixteenth Street Baptist Church, rising in the background, along with the Birmingham Civil Rights Institute and Kelly Ingram Park have all contributed. Interestingly enough, the Poole Funeral Chapel, which has been in this location since 1952, now anchors the block. Located at 1501 Seventh Avenue North, a few lots to the east of the old Bradford Funeral Home's previous location, the Poole Funeral Chapel now serves the community. Instead of a row of residences and the funeral home, most of the lots along Seventh Avenue—including the Bradford Funeral Home site—are now vacant, victims of urban decay.

The Joy Young Restaurant, located across the street from the old Tutwiler Hotel on Twentieth Street North, was Birmingham's signature downtown Chinese restaurant. In this 1937 photo taken by the Birmingham View Company, the establishment advertises on the neon sign special offerings such as "Sea Foods," "Chop Suey," and private booths for customers' use. While the restaurant previously occupied two other downtown locations, it was here in this prime spot across from the city's best-known hotel that it made its name. Opened as the King Joy Inn Restaurant years before, four partners established the landmark: Mansion Joe, Loo Bing, George Sai, and Loo Choy. Reportedly, the Joe family was the first Chinese family to settle in Alabama back in the 1880s. Three generations of the Joe family managed the restaurant.

Today, Wachovia Bank's Wachovia Tower (formerly SouthTrust Bank, which was formerly Birmingham Trust National Bank) has its Birmingham offices in this location. Completed in 1986, the thirty-four-story office tower is the city's tallest building at 454 feet. Sadly, the Joe Young Restaurant is no more. In October 1980, the restaurant moved from what was then a downtown in decline to the nearby suburb of Homewood, oddly relocating in a strip of businesses found under the parking deck of Brookwood Hospital. Such was the impact of the Joy Young Restaurant on Birmingham's consciousness that arbitrary references continue to surface in everyday conversation today—a recent political thriller, *The 28th Amendment* by Neal Rechtman, also refers to this landmark. The Chop Suey Inn, a Chinese restaurant located on Green Springs Highway in Homewood, reportedly serves what is the closest thing one can find to Joy Young's famous egg rolls.

Of all the historic structures now gone from Birmingham's physical landscape, the old Terminal Station is perhaps the most sorely missed. Opened in 1909 to better accommodate the growing city (due to annexations, Birmingham grew from 38,000 to 132,000 residents from 1900 to 1910), the massive $2 million Beaux Arts–style structure was designed by P. Thorton Mayre and was covered in light brown brick. The central waiting room was 7,600 square feet and was topped with a dome sixty-four feet in diameter, decorated with tile and topped by an ornamental glass skylight. In 1926 E. H. Eliott donated the large electric sign seen in this photograph to the city, and at the Terminal Station's west end, it became the city's de facto welcoming sign for generations of visitors arriving at the terminal. Interestingly, most popular postcards of the day reverse the "Magic City" sign to create a better effect. O. V. Hunt took this famous photo.

What remains today was called the "subway," or underpass, that the streetcar used to pass beneath the station while picking up or dropping off passengers. In 1969 the Terminal Station was demolished as part of a development scheme that never came to fruition. The numerous hotels, cafés, and entertainments along Fifth Avenue that welcomed visitors are gone. Today, part of the Red Mountain Expressway that connects Highways 31 and 280 with Interstates 20 and 59 travels over the former Terminal Station site, an ignominious if consistent use for what was once the central hub of Birmingham traffic and transportation before the era of rail travel was eclipsed by cars and airplanes. Park Place, a mixed-income development nearby, has revitalized the neighborhood.

Temple Emanu-El was founded by early Jewish settlers in 1882. Just four years later, the cornerstone of the first synagogue in the county was laid on the corner of Fifth Avenue and Seventeenth Street North. Rabbi Morris Newfield, a Hungarian immigrant, was chosen to lead the congregation in 1895, and over the next twenty years the congregation increased to more than 300 families, necessitating a larger facility. Newfield led Temple Emanu-El for the next forty-five years, during which time he oversaw the construction of the new temple in 1914 at its present location at 2100 Highland Avenue. Architect William C. Weston combined classic and Byzantine styles, topping the structure with a large bronze dome and portico supported by four Corinthian columns. Thick walls support the seventy-two-foot dome, which is itself supported by stress rather than structural steel.

The spiritual center for Reform Jews in the Birmingham area, Temple Emanu-El added an educational building in 1955 that adjoins the original structure. Designed by W. N. Chambers, it is named in honor of Rabbi Newfield. In 2002 a $17 million campaign to renovate and repair the temple was completed, with additional funds being used to further build its endowment. The modern facility, with its dark steel and glass components, makes a marked and appealing contrast to the tan brick of the original structure. The temple has a membership of more than 750 families and is active in the local community in programs such as P.E.A.C.E. Birmingham.

Built in 1913, the Molton Hotel stood on the corner of Fifth Avenue and Twentieth Street, just across from the Tutwiler Hotel. Like the Redmont and Bankhead hotels, all were on Fifth Avenue to access the direct connection from the Terminal Station where numerous passengers disembarked daily. Thomas Henry Morton, founder of the Molton Realty Company, oversaw the construction of the hotel, which was designed by Charles Wheelock.

A beautiful eight-story, 122-foot structure with Italian Renaissance details, it was of brown brick with terra-cotta trim. This photo from the 1920s shows the hotel in its prime. Though his hotel was constructed before the Tutwiler, Molton refused to open it until after the rival hotel so that he could advertise the Molton Hotel as "Birmingham's newest hotel."

Years later, a 1940s Molton Hotel advertisement would continue to boast, claiming the best-ventilated rooms in the South. The hotel was still owned by the Molton family when it was demolished in 1979. Today, the pink granite headquarters of Compass Bank, which is owned by Spain's Banco Bilbao Vizcaya Argentaria, occupies the same corner. Completed in 1982, the seventeen-story building was designed by the architectural firm of

Giattina, Fisher and Company. While Compass is the anchor tenant in the building, the Birmingham Chamber of Commerce offices are in the same location. The intersection, which once held two of the city's most prominent hotels, had, by the 1980s, become the banking center for Birmingham, a shift that reflected the city's rise as a regional financial center.

Seen in this striking photograph taken a year after its completion in 1925, the Alabama Power Company Building at the corner of Sixth Avenue and Eighteenth Street North towers over the smaller buildings and few remaining homes in the vicinity. Designed by the architectural firm of Warren, Knight, and Davis, the fourteen-story structure is dramatically crowned by a twenty-three-foot golden statue of Electra, and features limestone and terra-cotta trim. Framing the main entrance are three ten-foot statues carved by Edward Field Sanford Jr. that represent power, light, and heat. London's *Daily Express* called the building "one of the three most beautiful public utility buildings in the world," and it is certainly the greatest Art Deco–style structure in Birmingham. In the distance, the two domes of the Sixteenth Street Baptist Church can be seen.

Founded in 1906 in Gadsden, Alabama, the Alabama Power Company is today the second-largest division of the Southern Company and is an investor-owned public utility. Its headquarters are still located in this building in downtown Birmingham, though now a complex of additional structures comprise the headquarters. A twelve-story annex was built on the rear of the building along Sixth Avenue in 1951, and in 1957 an eight-story annex was built on Eighteenth Street. More construction followed in 1966 in the location of the old Henley School when the fleet parking deck was built. The most recent project at this site was the new eighteen-story tower and parking deck completed in 1988. In this photo, Alabama Power is finishing general preservation and restoration work on its building.

Adolf Loveman opened a dry-goods emporium in Birmingham in 1887, and consistently expanded his business over the next few decades. Shortly after he died in 1916, the Loveman, Joseph, and Loeb store seen in the small inset photo from the 1920s became one of the largest department stores in the city. After a fire gutted the building in 1934, a new store was built in the same location at the corner of Third Avenue North and Nineteenth Street. It was reputed to be the first department store in the nation to be air-conditioned and the first in the state to feature an escalator. This 1936 photograph from across the street at the Kress Building shows local workers indulging in some lunchtime shopping.

Loveman's closed its doors in 1980, and with it an era of downtown shopping and commerce passed. Suitably, the building was placed on the National Register of Historic Places in 1983 but stood empty for years until the McWane Science Center renovated and expanded the building, combining the Red Mountain Museum and the Discovery Place institutions in one location. The museum collections are of special interest, and the Alabama Collections Center houses numerous artifacts unearthed during the construction of the Red Mountain Expressway, such as a large collection of mosasaurs (extinct marine lizards) and other fossils. The nonprofit science museum and a research archive opened in 1998 and has more than 9,000 square feet of interactive exhibits. A science center, aquarium, and 280-seat IMAX Dome Theater are housed in the old store. Many attribute this redevelopment as a turning point in downtown Birmingham's revitalization. The center is named after the McWane family and McWane, Inc., which helped fund the center.

This frenetic, energized scene from May 1, 1898, shows recruits gathered at the Louisville and Nashville Railroad Station on Morris Avenue getting ready to depart aboard a special train bound for Miami and then Cuba, to fight in the Spanish-American War. Bands were playing and older Confederate veterans greeted the young soldiers. Some 700 recruits from the vicinity signed up to serve their nation. The Woodlawn Light Infantry (nicknamed "Hidgon's Hobos" for their colonel, Elijah L. Higdon), the Bessemer Rifles, East Lake's Huey Guards, and the Pratt City's Clark Rifles completed Jefferson County's recruits in the First Alabama Division. Company F, led by Lieutenant Dabney Luckie, joined the "colored regiment" known as the Third Alabama. They didn't make it to Cuba before the war was over, but by then the ravages of the southern Florida heat, dysentery, and typhoid had taken its own toll. Most returned home in the fall to equally enthusiastic crowds. The 1871 Relay House, a two-story wooden hotel built by the Elyton Land Company, previously stood here until 1886.

Listed in the National Register of Historic Places, Morris Avenue and First Avenue North have been recognized for their many warehouses located in the 2200–2400 blocks of Morris and the 2100–2500 blocks of First Avenue North. Morris Avenue is a popular spot for photographers who want to capture the cobblestone streets and quaint storefronts, just out of frame to the left of this view. *Ravagers*, staring Richard Harris, Ernest Borgnine, and Art Carney, was staged there in the late 1970s. The railroad line is now elevated over

Twentieth Street and the streetcar lines, electrified back in 1891, were taken up or paved over in the 1950s. First American Bank has offices across the street from where the station used to be, a corner that now houses HKW Associates, based on the ground floor of the seventeen-story Two North Twentieth Building. It was formerly the Bank for Savings Building, the first significant building constructed in downtown Birmingham since the Depression.

This lovely whimsical building, built in 1920 by architect William Leslie Welton, has touches of Spanish Colonial influences in the spiral-fluted columns at the entrances along with blue-glazed terra-cotta arches. A parapet with gables covers the roof, and the tenth floor has Palladian windows with arches at the corners. Built at the site of a fruit stand at Twentieth Street and Third Avenue North, the original plan called for a five-story building to house real-estate developer Richard W. Massey's business college. He expanded to ten floors with the intent to lease the Banker's Bond Company the first five floors, naming the building after the bond company; however, after the company failed in the Great Depression, the structure soon bore Massey's name.

Today, the 65,000-square-foot historic building is typically at 100 percent occupancy, no doubt due to its location downtown as well as its notable exterior. When it was constructed, it stood across the corner from the old Jefferson County Courthouse, an equally desirable location. A group of the partners in the law firm of Hare, Wynn, Newell and Newton purchased the building in 1990 and completely renovated seven of the ten floors. While the majority of the building is leased to law firms, Moe's Original BBQ is the newest tenant. In 1911 when Richard Massey was president of the Birmingham Chamber of Commerce, a special celebration was held in recognition of the city's rapid growth. In his speech, Massey used the term "magic citizens" for the people of Birmingham. He also called Birmingham the "Magic City, a city of perpetual promise." The term stuck, and the city had its moniker.

Dated May 15, 1915, this photo of an elaborate formal meal being enjoyed in the main dining room of the Bright Star restaurant is sometimes attributed as the first meal served in the venerable establishment. That is unlikely, given that it moved to this site in Bessemer in 1914 after outgrowing its previous location, a small café with a horseshoe-shaped bar that opened in 1907. With its intricate tiled floor, mirrored walls, decorative marble, and the ceiling fans so necessary prior to the advent of air-conditioning, the Bright Star was an elegant, refined culinary destination in the booming town of Bessemer. Located at 304 Nineteenth Street North, Bessemer's "Main Street," the Bright Star was founded by Tom Bonduris. In 1923 brothers Pete and Bill Koikos, recent immigrants from Greece, purchased an ownership in the restaurant.

Today, Jim and Nick Kiokos, Bill's sons, run the landmark restaurant, having taken over the reins in 1966—a visit for their popular "meat-and-three" lunch is complete after a welcoming nod or greeting from one of the brothers. Since the 1960s, the restaurant and its kitchen have been completely altered and renovated, expanding to 330 seats with banquet rooms and private dining options, but the heart of the place remains the central dining room with its

romantic murals painted by an itinerant European artist. The restaurant is well known for its Greek-style snapper and broiled chicken, seafood gumbo, and a host of fresh vegetables. Many mealtimes have turned into delightful chaos as patrons argue over what pie to share: lemon icebox, coconut cream, pineapple cheese, or peanut butter. The last expansion in 1985 created the Dixie and Green rooms.

For a young city like Birmingham (not yet fifty years old in this photo), trying to compete with nearby cities such as Nashville, Atlanta, and Chattanooga was a constant challenge. Unwarranted accolades—such as George Cruikshank's remark in his *A History of Birmingham* in 1920 that Birmingham was "the industrial stronghold of America"—were not uncommon for the time. Yet beyond the Magic City moniker, perhaps the most enduring and imaginative boilerplates describing a part of the city was one given to the intersection of Twentieth Street and First Avenue North. The term "Heaviest Corner on Earth" came into prominence when four of the taller buildings in the region—from left to right, the sixteen-story Empire Building (1909), sixteen-story Brown Marx Building (1906), twenty-one-story American Trust and Savings Bank Building (1912), and the ten-story Woodward Building (1902)—were constructed around the same time in this location. The photo, taken by O. V. Hunt circa 1921, is probably the most iconic picture of this intersection. At far right, the Britling cafeteria marquee can be seen above this popular local institution.

An article entitled "Birmingham to Have the Heaviest Corner in the South" ran in the *Jemison Magazine* in 1911. Proper, if exaggerated, civic boosterism may be the routine domain of chambers of commerce, yet this remark stuck in the spirit of good local color and flair. In a short time, the exaggeration became bolder and the term "Heaviest Corner on Earth" became part of the local parlance. In 1985 the Birmingham Historical Society and Operation New Birmingham claimed it once and for all, placing a marker on the sidewalk outside of the Empire Building that elaborates on the moniker. A few months later that same year, the "Heaviest Corner on Earth" was added to the National Register of Historic Places, proof that if you repeat something often enough, it becomes fact.

Established in 1871 on a twenty-one-acre plot of land purchased from the Elyton Land Company, Oak Hill Cemetery is Birmingham's most distinguished cemetery. Almost every notable city founder, politician, developer, or industrialist was interred in Oak Hill Cemetery. Prior to being purchased by the city, it was marked "City Cemetery" on the first plans produced for Birmingham. It was sold to the city in 1873 for $1,073.50, yet had already been used as a burial ground for the previous owner's infant daughter in 1869. The first grave dated is that of Jesse Thompson, the father of Birmingham's fifth mayor. This photo from 1927 shows a monument to Mortimer H. Jordan, commander of the Sixteenth Infantry, Forty-Second Division in the "Rainbow Division" in World War I.

Taken from behind the Pioneer's Memorial Building—an attractive Gothic structure built of Indiana limestone and designed by Miller and Martin, Architects—this photo shows how little Oak Hill has changed. The main differences are the removal of shrubbery, the signs of pollution marking the formerly white statues, and the unfortunate vandalism that resulted in the loss of Jesus's head from the Hopkins memorial. Maintained by the Oak Hill Memorial Association, a nonprofit group that has maintained the historic cemetery since 1913, it is open to the public from 8:00 a.m. to 4:00 p.m. during the week for self-guided tours. Visitors are encouraged, and guided tours are also available when scheduled in advance. In 2004 the association contracted with experts in cemetery conservation to solicit recommendations for a master preservation plan for the site.

When George B. Ward, mayor of Birmingham (1905–1909 and 1913–1914), completed his home on Shades Mountain in 1925, it became an overnight sensation. Costing $200,000, the eccentric design replicates the Temple of the Vestal Virgins in the Roman Forum. Twenty Doric columns supported the four-story circular building of pink sandstone. Four years later, Ward constructed this Temple of Sibyl, which dramatically overlooked the valley below. It was modeled after a similar temple at Tivoli, Italy. Elaborately staged photos of sylvan nymphs frolicking in their gauzy gowns not long after its completion only further enflamed the curiosity of nearby residents. Until Birmingham's other mountaintop attraction (Vulcan) was established a decade later, Ward's bachelor pad had very little competition for scenic curiosity with a view.

Following World War II, the new subdivision with a view of Red Mountain in the distance took the name Vestavia Hills in honor of Ward's creation. After the Vestavia Hills Baptist Church demolished Ward's old home in 1971 to make room for a new sanctuary, only the Temple of Sibyl remained from this remarkable landmark. Through the work of the Vestavia Hills Garden Club as well as the Harbert Construction Company, the temple was preserved and moved to its location at the top of Highway 31 in 1975. The process was arduous, to say the least. The dome itself weighs more than sixty tons and is supported by Corinthian columns. The foundation comprises marble salvaged from the Tutwiler Hotel before it was demolished around the same time. Today, with recent renovations and landscaping improvements, the Temple of Sibyl and its view of Vulcan in the distance currently enjoy what is arguably their best condition since Ward first built his home.

Birmingham's first high school was essentially the graduating class from nearby Powell School. In 1906 the city built this high school at Seventh Avenue and Twenty-fourth Street. Locals alternately called it Central High or Birmingham High School as well as simply "the high school." This photograph from 1910 shows the school before it burned down in 1918. Phillips High School replaced the structure in 1923 and enrolled nearly 3,000 students from the central part of the city. Designed by the firm Breeding and Whilldin, Phillips is a fine example of the progressive educational reforms of this period. It is named for John Herbert Phillips, Birmingham's first superintendent of schools.

After the newly constructed Carver High School took over as the city's main high school in 2001, Phillips became a professional development center as well as a resource for other city schools undergoing renovations. For a time, the Alabama Historical Commission placed the school on its "Places in Peril" list. In 2007, after $9 million in renovations, middle school grades holding classes here are known as the John Herbert Phillips Academy. As a K-8 educational center and teaching laboratory, the greater facility is intended to be a magnet school for students throughout the city. Phillips High School's most notorious moment came in 1957 when Fred Shuttlesworth, president of the Alabama Christian Movement for Human Rights, attempted to integrate the school with four black children and their parents. His attempts were met with violence by a Klan-led mob, and it wasn't until federal intervention in 1964 that the school was finally integrated.

In 1920 a group began organizing a Baptist church in Edgewood, purchasing two lots on the present site. Five years later, Edgewood Baptist Church (now known as Dawson Memorial Baptist Church) formed and invited Lemuel O. Dawson to be the first pastor, holding service in Shades Cahaba High School. Dawson, a professor at Howard College, helped the young congregation raise $3,500, which—along with an $11,000 loan—constructed what was known as the Fieldstone Building. Designed by George P. Nelson, the architect responsible for most of the early Spanish Colonial–style homes built in nearby Hollywood, this beautiful, almost quaint structure, reminiscent of an English country church, opened in December 1925. The Edgewood Electric Railway line, which linked with the South Highland streetcar line in downtown Birmingham, ran along Manhattan Street and connected the church with the greater community. This photo, which shows the newly completed Dawson looming behind the Fieldstone Building, was taken in the early 1950s just before the old sanctuary's demolition.

After World War II, Dawson Memorial Baptist Church saw a dramatic upswing in attendance and a war surplus army chapel from Tuskegee was purchased to temporarily ease the postwar strain. In the late 1940s, the church had George P. Nelson design a new, larger sanctuary that cost $200,000 to construct. Further expansion came across Manhattan Street to the north and Oxmoor Road to the south, prompting some controversy and protests by the Homewood Citizens Association, which was concerned about the church's growth in the early 1980s—ironically, expansion has only increased since then. Some of the more recent additions include the Family Recreation Center (1999), the four-story parking deck (2005), and the North Building renovation of existing offices and classrooms, completed in 2005. Today, Dawson's average weekly attendance is approximately 2,500.

RED MOUNTAIN

Taken in 1909 by the Birmingham View Company, a new commercial photography studio that provided commissioned images for their clients, this photograph shows the freshly surfaced road that meandered along the south side of Red Mountain. One of the few routes "over the mountain" to Shades Valley in the distance, this byway already had the electric power lines running from downtown Birmingham over the ridge in the direction of fledgling communities such as Rosedale and Oak Grove. Around the same time, the Edgewood Highland Land Company bought 1,700 acres of Shades Valley, platting 200 acres of it under the name Edgewood. A short commute from the ritzy residential area of South Highland on the Southside, the idea was for this to be the primary route channeling the wealthiest citizens to outlying recreational opportunities as a shift was taking place from heavy industry to residential development.

The Edgewood Electric Railway began service to Lone Pine Gap in 1911 after dynamiting a seventy-foot-deep cut at the crest of Red Mountain. The *Birmingham News* called the new line "a landmark in the progress and growth of this city." Some three decades after the previous photo was taken, a much-improved and largely unrecognizable Twentieth Street South became the route that U.S. Highway 31 took over Red Mountain down to the community of Homewood. By the end of the 1940s, the streetcar tracks were removed and the route became the domain of automobiles. The old Valley View Mine resides nearby under what is today Vulcan Park, seen at right in this photo.

Birmingham's creation is very much a parable of the industrial age. After the Civil War, the area around Jones Valley was known to be rich in the minerals and resources needed to make iron. James Withers Sloss, a merchant and investor, convinced the Louisville and Nashville Railroad to complete the rail line through the valley, effectively jump-starting the town. In 1880 he founded the Sloss Furnace Company. As pig iron production grew, there were nineteen furnaces in Jefferson County alone. By World War I, Sloss-Sheffield Steel and Iron (as it was renamed) was one of the largest pig iron producers in the world. By World War II, nearly half of Birmingham's workforce was in the iron, steel, and mining industries—and more than two-thirds of these workers were African American—making Birmingham a remarkably segregated and stratified city. This nighttime photo of the Number Two furnaces was probably taken in the 1940s. The glow is from the slag field.

After producing iron from 1882 to 1971, the Sloss furnaces became a National Historic Landmark, one of the first such early industrial sites to be so recognized. When the furnaces closed and preliminary plans to convert the site to a museum of industry faltered, the furnaces were slated to be demolished. A public outcry followed, and by 1983 a modest museum had opened. It is currently the only twentieth-century blast furnace preserved as a historic site. Currently, a master site plan is being developed to house a visitor center and exhibit gallery. This view of one of Sloss's two 400-ton blast furnaces is taken from the viaduct at First Avenue North. The exhaust stack can be seen in the distance (now with the bell at the top removed), along with the boilers, stoves, and old slag pit in front of the casting shed.

Named in honor of the American Legion, the stadium at 400 Graymont Avenue was completed in 1927 at a cost of $439,000. Sometimes called the "Old Gray Lady," its capacity at the time of this 1931 photo was 21,000. The first game of college football played at the stadium was between Howard College (now Samford University) and Birmingham–Southern College. The imposing limestone sculptures of sleeping lions at the formal south entrance to the field flank a memorial placed by the Birmingham American Legion Post No. 1 in 1929. Bronze plaques list those military personnel from Alabama who died in World War I. Photographer O. V. Hunt took this picture of Birmingham's motorcycle officers for the Firestone Tire and Rubber Company and Gail Joyce Motor Company.

Much has obviously changed in the intervening decades. Legion Field became most famous as the site of the Alabama-Auburn football game known as the "Iron Bowl." Each year from 1948 to 1988, the fierce rivalry was held here, as were various bowl games and several failed incarnations of professional football leagues. The stadium added an upper deck in 1961, a modern press box in 1965, and lights in 1969. Recent removal of the upper deck for safety reasons reduced its seating to just over 70,000. Ironically enough, the stadium's greatest capacity (83,810) was achieved during the 1996 Olympics for a soccer match between the United States and Argentina.

By the late 1880s, the Birmingham Coal Barons baseball team was playing in a baseball park called the "Old Slag Pile" on First Avenue near Fourteenth Street. But when Allen Harvey "Rick" Woodward purchased the minor league club in 1909, the local baseball scene was set to change. After consulting with player-manager Connie Mack for advice, Woodward modeled his new Rickwood Field on Forbes Field in Pittsburgh. Built for $75,000, the new stadium in West End went on to host both the Birmingham Barons and the

Birmingham Black Barons of the Negro Southern League, as well as stalwarts of the game such as Ty Cobb, Babe Ruth, "Shoeless" Joe Jackson, Dizzy Dean, Satchel Paige, and of course, Willie Mays, who grew up just outside of Birmingham. This photo shows the sixth and final game in the annual Dixie Series in 1929. The Barons beat the champions from the Texas League 7–5 to clinch the series. A year earlier, a Mission-style facade over the main entrance was constructed, adding additional glamour to the park.

The 10,800-seat Rickwood Field is today the world's oldest surviving baseball park. In fact, it is arguably the closest one can get to the passion and excitement of baseball's glory days, seen in the many baseball movies filmed here, such as *Cobb* and *Soul of the Game*. In this image, one can see that the dugouts have been relocated to the outside of the tunnel and lowered to below field level. The most significant change to the park occurred in 1987 when the Birmingham Barons relocated to a new facility, Metropolitan Stadium (currently known as Regions Park), in the suburb of Hoover. Since 1992 the Friends of Rickwood, a nonprofit group, has raised more than $2 million to maintain and restore the historic site. Today, the Rickwood Classic, an annual game played in period uniforms, continues the field's great tradition, as do other amateur and semiprofessional games and events held here.

Built in 1822 by Stephen Hall on his 475-acre property, Arlington began as an unpretentious home with two upstairs rooms and two downstairs rooms. The grandeur seen in this photo is largely due to William S. Mudd, a circuit court judge who purchased the property at a public auction in 1842. Mudd added an east wing and the facade, turning the home into an eight-room Greek Revival mansion facing north. For all practical purposes, it was a new house. Square columns support the low-pitched hip roof that is bound by four

two-story brick chimneys. Inside, the halls run from the front to the back of the building on both floors, and the hall on the second floor opens to a veranda in the back of the house. Commandeered by Union General James Wilson during the Civil War, Arlington was fortunate to survive. Located at the center of old Elyton, the first permanent county seat for Jefferson County, the mansion has long been a landmark.

In 1953 fifty prominent citizens purchased the house and grounds from the Montgomery family and deeded it to the City of Birmingham to make what is now known as Arlington Antebellum Home and Gardens, a center for cultural and historical activities. As such, today it is the oldest building in the city and the second-oldest museum. Both the original chimneys and columns remain. The beautifully manicured lawns and gardens make the old structure a popular site for weddings, receptions, and various civic events. Robert Munger bought the home at the turn of the century, and around 1910 he added trees to replace the cedar, oak, and ash that Mudd previously planted. Munger used Arlington as a summer retreat, and the grounds and gardens that used to reflect his Edwardian sensibilities now exhibit a more stylized feel. Today, many of the flowers are laid out almost exactly as Munger would have known them.

Built in 1924 and designed in consultation with Thomas W. Lamb, a noted theater architect, the Municipal Auditorium was the first city structure built on the government campus surrounding Woodrow Wilson Park (now Linn Park). Constructed of red brick, it was a striking building, with touches of Lombard influences seen in the arched corbels on the gable. In this photograph, one can see a sign announcing the "All Southern Concert and Fiddler's Contest," just one of many events held here in 1948, which included political conventions, festivals, Broadway plays, musical concerts, Ku Klux Klan rallies, car shows, and the States' Rights Party convention. Other pivotal events held here include the Southern Conference for Human Welfare in 1938 that joined white and black progressives working for a more equitable society. That integrated affair featured a dramatic showdown between First Lady Eleanor Roosevelt and Birmingham City Commissioner T. Eugene "Bull" Connor over audience segregation.

Renamed to honor former Birmingham mayor Albert Boutwell, the auditorium underwent a major facelift in 1957. Architect Charles McCauley added a lobby and other rooms in front of the original brick facade, obscuring the front entrance's more classical style with his modernist design of marble, glass, and aluminum. The red brick has also been painted, again utterly transforming the look of the structure from the front. Continuing Boutwell's history of hosting controversial and notable cultural events, it caught the national media's attention when Birmingham Pride Alabama organized a screening of the TV sitcom *Ellen* when the local ABC affiliate refused to broadcast the episode featuring the title character's "coming out" as a lesbian. Proposals put forth in 2007 by the mayor of Birmingham to demolish the structure are pending.

Originally the central U.S. post office of Birmingham, the U.S. Treasury Department designed this Classical Revival–style structure in 1916, but World War I interfered with its construction. It was completed in 1921, just a few years before this photo was taken. Oscar Wilder Underwood, a senator from Alabama and the Senate minority leader at the time of the post office's construction, helped ensure the structure was large enough for the rapidly growing city. Almost monumental in size with a long row of Ionic columns, the building takes up half a city block. It is built of white Georgia marble, and both the windows and entrances on the first floor have arches.

In 1990 the building was renamed the Robert Smith Vance Federal Building and Courthouse in honor of the circuit court judge killed by a mail bomb in 1989—only the third United States federal judge to have been murdered as a result of his service. Located at 1800 Fifth Avenue North, the building is listed on the National Register of Historic Places. Behind it one can see the newer Alabama Power buildings, as well as the AT&T Building (formerly the BellSouth Building). In order to admit more traffic lanes along Eighteenth Street, parking has been eliminated on the east side of the street and the diagonal parking shifted to parallel parking on the west side adjacent to the courthouse.

Quite the entrepreneur, Richard W. Massey was a businessman and educator who, after arriving in Birmingham in 1887 with meager means, soon parlayed his modest Massey Business College for farmers into a network of business colleges throughout the Southeast. His forays into real-estate development paid off handsomely as well, and by 1905 he owned one of the city's most envied homes along Twenty-first Way South. His formal Italian gardens were replete with fountains, pools, and statuary, and were cared for by European gardeners. This photo from the 1910 *Birmingham De Luxe* book was used as the basis for a postcard later published by the Birmingham Post Card Exchange. One can just make out the open-top auto with passengers in the driveway at left. Massey was one of the first to relocate to Robert Jemison's Mountain Brook Estates development south of the city, constructing a large Spanish-style home on Mountain Brook Parkway.

Unfortunately, the magnificent Massey estate was torn down to make way for the Elton B. Stephens Expressway, known locally as the Red Mountain Expressway (or, more simply, "the Cut"). Located off to the right in this photo, Massey's home was part of the right-of-way that connected Highways 31 and 280 to Interstates 20 and 59 at this north-south corridor—author Walker Percy's family home was another casualty of the freeway. Named for the local philanthropist who chaired the committee, the expressway's construction began in 1962 with the blasting of the cut. An overpass along Highland Avenue, where this photo was taken, was finalized in 1967, and the expressway opened in 1970, much to the joy of commuters from Homewood, Mountain Brook, Vestavia, and other suburbs who drove into downtown for work. For a time, the Red Mountain Museum, a small science museum on the east side of the cut, displayed the wealth of fossils and geological finds the expressway revealed.

The history of St. Vincent's has in many ways mirrored that of Birmingham. When the wild, young city was in desperate need of a hospital, Father Patrick O'Reilly and two members of the Daughters of Charity of St. Vincent de Paul came to town from St. Louis in 1898. St. Vincent's initially was housed in the Henry DeBardeleben mansion until ground was broken on a completely new building that cost $223,000 a year later. A new east wing quickly followed in 1911 to ease the crowded hospital as Birmingham grew by 20 percent during the first decade of the new century. Since that time, St. Vincent's growth and expansion has mirrored Birmingham's, in good times and bad. This photo from around 1915 was taken when the facility had approximately twenty-nine physicians, three interns, and fifty student nurses working with the eighteen sisters. The open porches off each floor offered fresh breezes, certainly a welcome feature before air-conditioning.

The lovely old building was demolished in 1972 to make way for its replacement—Professional Building One. The growth that the St. Vincent's Health System has seen is remarkable, and in addition to this large, sprawling complex in Birmingham, the system has four additional facilities: St. Vincent's Blount, St. Vincent's East, St. Vincent's St. Clair, and One Nineteen Health and Wellness. The facility added a 300-car parking deck in 1979, a new west wing in 1981, new professional buildings in 1988 and 2002, a cancer center in 1988, another parking deck for 800 cars in 1990, and a conference center in 1997. Most recently, a new Women's and Children's Center, seen in this view along Eighth Avenue, was completed with the Eleanor E. Kidd Rotunda as the centerpiece. In front of it stands the "Sisters' Vigil," a bronze sculpture representing the nuns who founded St. Vincent's. Today, the Catholic hospital complex has 338 licensed beds.

Located in the iron ore and limestone district in the southern part of Jones Valley, Bessemer was founded in the late 1880s by Henry DeBardeleben, who named it after Sir Henry Bessemer, the inventor of the Bessemer process for smelting iron. As a foil to Birmingham, the steelmaking city's moniker became "the Marvel City" for its rapid growth—for a time in the early 1900s, the city enjoyed the eighth-largest population in the state. The Bessemer Coal, Iron, and Land Company purchased a 4,000-acre town site and began laying it out by blocks in 1886. This early 1900s view along Second Avenue looking northeast between Eighteenth and Nineteenth streets shows the Grand Hotel, the Berney Block in the center, and the Charleston Block at the right. The Grand Hotel, the three-story building at left, was an Italianate-style building constructed in 1888 and was the city's social center for decades.

Marjorie L. White of the Birmingham Historical Society called these three blocks on Second Avenue "the finest remaining concentration of Victorian commercial architecture in the Birmingham District" in 1981. Sadly, they are no more. The Grand Hotel was torn down in the mid-1980s to make way for a sheriff's department building. And in 2007 the Charleston Block (later called the Steiner Block) was torn down to make way for a new courthouse designed by the Giattina Aycock Architecture Studio—seen during construction at right in this photo. The $38 million courthouse features 15,000 square feet of glass along the front. The county is also spending $11.2 million to add 19,000 square feet to the Bessemer jail across the street, which was built in 1988. It is a sign that Bessemer, a city that has seen hard times in the past decades, is undergoing something of a renaissance, albeit one that has meant the loss of a treasure.

Fed by water from the cool springs in the Roebuck area, East Lake made for a popular retreat from the heat of the city during the warm summer months. Developers created a thirty-three-acre lake within the new subdivision of East Lake in the late 1880s to promote the area, using concerts, vaudeville shows, and other entertainments to draw crowds. This photo from the early 1930s shows a crowded weekend scene at the amusement park. By this time, the City of Birmingham owned the park, and it featured water skiing, a Ferris wheel, shooting gallery, and other attractions. Many of the steel-industry workers in the neighborhood were of Italian descent, and so the lake was initially named "Como" after the resort destination in the Italian Alps.

Today, nearly all the buildings and structures from East Lake Park's heyday are gone, and the likelihood of seeing nearby residents frolicking in the old swimming hole is very small. Most visitors come to walk the park loop, cast a few lines angling for fish, or play golf at the nearby Don Hawkins Golf Course. The Family Fishing Rodeo, hosted annually by the Birmingham Park and Recreation Board, is the state's largest community fishing event. The old bathhouse, now known as the Shepherd Center (inset), adjoins the pool and is about the only structure remaining from the park's heyday. Designed by George P. Turner, it was built in the French Norman style and financed by the city bond issue of 1931.

Enoch Ensley, a wealthy planter from Memphis, purchased lands in Jefferson County in the early 1880s and intended to develop them during the iron boom in nearby Birmingham. After incorporating in 1899, the city quickly grew from less than 600 residents to more than 10,000 in two years. By 1907 some 14,000 men were working in the Ensley steel mills. This photo from the 1950s of a low-income neighborhood near the United States Steel Works in Ensley was shot for a *Time* magazine article and is revealing: the pipes of the mill physically tower over the town, representing the sole reason for the town's existence and development. The inset photo shows downtown from the corner of Avenue E and Nineteenth Street looking north. The Belle Theatre can be seen a block away on the left, along with other thriving businesses such as the Keith Furniture Company and the Lewis Mercantile Company.

After World War II, Ensley revived economically until U.S. Steel focused its operations in neighboring Fairfield. Nearly as haunting as the previous photo from this spot is the modern view of the skeletal remains of a once-great Birmingham steel industry. Seen in this photo of Twenty-second Street between Avenues E and D at the approximate location of the *Time* magazine photo, the city's decline is evident—yet even today, members of this close-knit community have remained loyal to the town and their roots. Ensley's

ten-story Ramsay-McCormack Tower, built in 1929 and seen at the far right in the inset photo, was the only substantial office building constructed outside of downtown Birmingham before the 1950s. An Art Deco treasure, it has been empty since 1986. Across the street, the distinctive granite-faced Bank of Ensley with its Ionic pilasters was built in 1919, just after the previous inset photo was taken.

Located in Ensley where the Wylam and Pratt City streetcar lines cross, this two-block neighborhood made famous in big-band leader Erskine Hawkins's 1939 song "Tuxedo Junction" was the social and entertainment hub of Birmingham's black community from the 1920s to the 1950s. Located at the intersection of Ensley Avenue and Twentieth Street, the area was known locally as the Junction, a place where the predominantly black communities of Fairfield, Ensley, Wylam, Bush Hills, and Pratt City would gather for dancing and to hear live music such as jazz, swing, and the blues. The Nixon Building, seen in this 1972 photo, was built in 1922 and held a second-floor dance hall that was one of the few places where black people could gather socially. The ground floor was originally separated into a market and the dental offices of Dr. Andrew Belcher. The weathered inset photo from 1939 is one of the few remaining from the club's heyday.

At the height of the club's success, the Nixon Building hosted an array of talented musicians such as Lionel Hampton (who, like Erskine Hawkins, grew up in the neighborhood), Urbie Green (a local studio musician), B. B. King, Ella Fitzgerald, and Nat "King" Cole. Paul Williams and Eddie Kendricks, founding members of the Temptations, also honed their skills in the Junction. The juke joints, eateries, and bars are gone today, but a historic marker commemorates the community's musical heritage. The sidewalks around the empty Nixon Building are inlaid with musical notes and there's a collage marking the spot of what was once a popular nightclub. Every summer during the last weekend of July, the City of Birmingham and the Erskine Hawkins Foundation hold the "Function in the Junction" festival one block east of the Nixon Building where one just might hear the lyrics "Way down south in Birmingham / I mean south in Alabam' / There's a place where people go / To dance the night away."

The Birmingham Municipal Airport Terminal opened in style on May 31, 1931, on a 315-acre site five miles east of the city. The administration building, seen here looking toward the hangar, illustrates the exclusivity and elegance that air travel promised at the time. Built in a grand Colonial style, the "sky harbor," as it was called, featured ticket booths, a passenger waiting room, and a restaurant. A second-story balcony was a popular spot for watching aircraft takeoffs and landings. The first commercial service was a stop by American Airways on its Atlanta–Fort Worth route.

Demolished in the 1950s to expand and modernize the airport facility, the stately old buildings are long gone—as is the glamour of air travel, one might argue. While a high state tax on aviation fuel slowed growth for a time in the late 1950s, the airport's expansion has been steady since then. In 1993 a $50 million terminal renovation, seen here, was completed. In 2001 a new 211-foot FAA control tower was finished. In 1986, when the Birmingham Airport Authority was organized independently of the City of Birmingham to administer the facility, only thirty-eight daily flights were offered. By 2000 more than three million passengers were served with eighty-one daily departures. Today, the facility is known as the Birmingham International Airport.

In the 1890s, the town of Owenton, located just west of Birmingham, was chosen by a committee of the First Methodist Church of Birmingham as the site for a new college. Rose Wellington Owen donated the land. From its hilltop perch, Owen Hall overlooked Jones Valley and was the site of the first building of the North Alabama Conference College, also known as Owenton College. After becoming part of Birmingham, the area became known as College Hills. Dr. Anson West, a member of the committee advocating the construction of the college, and one of its strongest supporters, became its fourth president. He is quoted as saying, "God created that hill for the site of a college." The cornerstone for Rose Owen Hall was laid in 1897, and Owen College opened the following year. This photo was taken around 1910.

When Southern University of Greensboro, Alabama, merged with Owenton College on May 30, 1918, the consolidated institution was called Birmingham–Southern College. Robert S. Munger, another staunch supporter of Owenton College in the early twentieth century, gave both his money and personal time to improving the young institution. During World War I, Owen Hall was used as a barracks for soldiers. The old hall was demolished in 1927 to build Munger Memorial Hall. Today, the hall is home to the office of the president and provost as well as the finance and human resources departments. The campus has grown from that initial sixteen acres donated at its founding to 192 acres today and has forty-five buildings, twenty-five of which are either new or have been renovated since 1976.

Built by Homewood developer Clyde Nelson in 1926, the private social club was located along the Shades Valley Highway. Designed in the Spanish Mission style prevalent in the Hollywood neighborhood, the clubhouse held a large swimming pool with a sandy beach area that was popular with teens and children. A ballroom and bandstand was the focal point of dances and gatherings. Seen in this picture taken from Shades Mountain shortly after Club Rex—as it was then known—was constructed, the elegant structure predates much of the residential development around it. It served as an enticement for Birminghamians to move south of town and into the developing suburbs over Red Mountain, an allure captured in one of Nelson's clever slogans, "Your home will eventually be in Shades Valley—the sooner you buy your lot, the more money you will save."

Plans to build a golf course on the grounds never came to fruition, and like the nearby Edgewood Country Club, ownership of Rex Club changed hands many times around the Great Depression. In the 1940s, a double-sided, sixty-three-foot neon sign at the new bridge along the Montgomery Highway announced "HOLLYWOOD COUNTRY CLUB" to passing motorists, giving notice that that the newly refurbished club was open to business again. In the late 1970s, the club enjoyed another resurgence, this time as the Brothers Music Hall, managed by Dan Nolen and Tony Ruffino. It hosted local favorites Hotel as well as national acts such as the Police, Pat Benatar, Warren Zevon, Elvis Costello, the Ramones, Bob Marley, and others. A fire damaged the club in 1984, and it was torn down shortly thereafter. Today, it is the site of a Courtyard by Marriott, seen just beyond the large Brookwood Medical Center complex across Shades Creek Parkway/Lakeshore Drive.

Located in the South Highlands area, the Phoenix Club formed on April 21, 1883, and was the city's oldest and largest Jewish social club. Incorporated by the city's leading merchants, the club had many homes before locating in this brown-brick clubhouse in the South Highlands area. The building cost $50,000 and was built by a group whose mission was to "promote the moral, social, literary and educational advancement of its members and to connect more closely the bonds of friendship between them." This circa-1909 photo shows the club from the corner of South Twentieth Street and Fifteenth Avenue. Called the "social center of the Jewish people of Birmingham," the club held bridge parties, dances, and other activities. Leo K. Steiner was the Phoenix Club's first president.

Prominent families such as the Adlers, Marxes, Sakses, Burgers, Phillipses, Lovemans, and others belonged to the club in the early part of the century. In 1920 the Phoenix Club continued to be the social center of the Reformed Jews of Birmingham. Eventually, the Phoenix Club reorganized as the Hillcrest Club, adding golf facilities on ninety-two acres along Oxmoor Road in Homewood. In 1969 the property was sold to the Zamora Shrine Temple (today, it is the Palisades Shopping Center). Around the same time, the club merged with the Fairmont Club to form the Pine Tree Country Club in Irondale, which joined the Reform and Traditional Jewish communities in one social club. Today, the old Phoenix Club building—which occupies nearly a city block—is the Zydeco nightclub as well as home to several other small businesses.

Shown here in the 1940s, this corner of Seventeenth Street North and Third Avenue North has been home to several theaters. This photo was taken during its incarnation as the Birmingham Theatre, which billed itself as "the largest and finest colored theatre in the entire South." Originally built as a civic auditorium in 1890, the structure was converted into the Bijou Theatre in 1898 and went on to become one of the city's premier spots for vaudeville acts. It was said to hold as many as six performances per week as well as three matinees accompanied by an orchestra. Around 1915 it closed and later reopened as part of the Loew's vaudeville circuit. On the opposite corner stood the Orpheum Theatre. In the late 1920s, the building was extensively remodeled and became the Pantages Theatre. It became known as the Birmingham Theatre in 1946.

True to its tradition of constant change, the Birmingham Theatre lasted only four short postwar years. The era of vaudeville had passed. It was demolished in 1950 after being purchased by the Panta Corporation. An article from that time showing the razing of the structure called it "one of the finest theater buildings in the South." That may be an exaggeration, but the theater did last longer than many of its contemporaries. For many years, the space served as a parking lot. Now the site of a Citizens Trust Bank Alabama (formerly Citizens Federal Savings Bank), the corner today reflects Birmingham's regional banking prominence, second only to Charlotte, North Carolina, as a banking center. Founded in 1956 by legendary Birmingham businessman A. G. Gaston, the bank was part of an empire that included a construction company, funeral homes, radio stations, and the Booker T. Washington Insurance Company, located at the right in this photograph.

Seen here in 1912 during its construction, the American Trust and Savings Bank Building was, at 284 feet, the tallest building in Alabama upon completion. That honor lasted for a year until the twenty-seven-story Jefferson County Savings and Bank building, which held the record until 1972, surpassed it. Designed by William Leslie Welton, the Classic Revival–style structure is a treasure of intricate details, from the Corinthian columns and limestone exterior to the large cornice that caps the building. The rounded corner along the street intersection is another distinctive touch and encapsulates an elegant door that originally opened below a large pediment. The interior is lined with Sylacauga marble. Standing on the corner of Twentieth Street and First Avenue North, the building is one of the four buildings that make up the somewhat exaggerated "Heaviest Corner on Earth."

In the 1930s, the American Trust and Savings Bank merged with First National Bank, which subsequently made the building its headquarters. In 1970 the building was renamed to honor John A. Hand, president of First National, a growing entity that itself was later renamed AmSouth Bank (which in 2006 merged with Regions Bank). After AmSouth moved its headquarters out of the building in the mid-1990s, the building was purchased at an auction and underwent a $20 million renovation by the McCrory Building Company to become the Superior Bank. Upper floors with their original woodwork and fixtures have been restored as luxury apartments. The City of Birmingham helped finance a $4.5 million parking deck across Morris Avenue behind the John A. Hand Building on Twentieth Street to support the new investment in the historic structure.

Located on the corner of First Avenue and Twentieth Street North, the sixteen-story Empire Building was built in 1909 on the former site of the Bank Saloon, a popular drinking parlor known for its thirty-two-foot mirror, which closed in 1908 during Birmingham's first "soft" prohibition. The lot itself was one of the first sold in Birmingham and originally went for $400. When the Empire Improvement Company, headed by Robert Jemison, purchased the land, they reportedly hired local architects William Welton and William Warren to design the building, though well-known architect J. E. R. Carpenter of New York was likely also involved. Until the John A. Hand Building was completed in 1912, it was the tallest structure in the state. This photograph from the 1920s shows the Saks department store, Steele-Smith department store, Chris Colias Café, Porter's Clothing Company, as well as the Greene Drug Company that for a time occupied the ground floor.

Some of the more striking elements of the neoclassical building are the entrance's large pink granite Doric columns and the exterior's molded terra-cotta facade on the sides facing the streets. The cornice has numerous large capital Es in homage to the developer, and the top three floors with their tall arched windows in the lavish Italian Renaissance style are literally the building's crowning achievement. In 1965 it was renamed the City National Bank Building when the bank formed that year, though locally it is primarily known as the Empire Building. Today, the building is owned by an Atlanta-based developer, which has announced plans to convert both the Empire and the Brown-Marx Tower across the street (together half of the "Heaviest Corner on Earth") into lofts. Colonial Bank currently occupies the building's ground floor, the only part of the building that is occupied.

Constructed in 1914 by Major Edward M. Tutwiler after he sold his Tutwiler Coal, Coke, and Iron Company, the lavish apartments were built the same year as the Tutwiler Hotel, an irony that would come full circle seven decades later. Eight stories tall, the brick structure at Twenty-first Street North and Park Place was designed by New York architect J. E. R. Carpenter to be the most luxurious apartments in Birmingham. During the early days, a rooftop garden was a popular gathering place for downtown residents. What is most revealing about this 1914 photo by O. V. Hunt taken just before its opening is the scale of the buildings surrounding the apartments. Just visible to the right are small, simple wooden homes, examples of a residential era that was quickly passing.

Although the heavy cornice around the roofline has been modified and most of the elegant balconies have been removed, the former apartments are almost as impressive today as they were nearly a century ago. When the original Tutwiler Hotel around the corner was imploded in 1974, the landmark seemed destined to vanish from the city landscape for good. However, the Tutwiler family still owned the Ridgely Apartments and a combination of $12 million in private funding and an $895,000 urban development grant in 1985 made possible the gutting of the old apartments and the creation of a new Tutwiler Hotel. Investor Harold Rosbottom purchased the hotel in 2006 and undertook a complete renovation. The $6.2 million project was completed in 2007, and today the hotel is part of Hampton Inn and Suites.

INDEX